Concept Learning in
the Social Studies
Models for Structuring Curriculum

Concept Learning in
the Social Studies
Models for Structuring Curriculum

PETER H. MARTORELLA

Temple University

INTEXT EDUCATIONAL PUBLISHERS
College Division
Scranton   Toronto   London

Consulting Editor

JOHN E. SEARLES
The Pennsylvania State University

ISBN 0–7002–2280–4

Library of Congress Catalog Card Number: 79-160674

To

CHRIS, TIM, and LAURA

All Super Concept Learners

Preface

Every book is based upon a fundamental premise, explicit or implicit. *This* book assumes that, to be optimally efficient, instructional procedures for the learning of *concepts* should be different from those used for other learning outcomes. In short, a teacher who wishes to teach a *concept* should follow a much different set of procedures or models than if he were attempting to teach a *generalization, skill,* or other specified objective.

Essentially what follows is the pursuit of this assumption: its clarification, including the nature of concepts; some implications of the assumption, including research findings and alternative models of instruction; and some tentative conclusions concerning the process of organizing instruction.

For those who wish to use the book primarily for direct classroom applications and who require as parsimonious a reading plan as possible, Parts One, Three, and Four should suffice. These sections, in the context of general methodology instruction, have been found to provide preservice, in-service, and workshop groups with sufficient understanding and direction to develop appropriate instructional materials. Part Two may be of greatest use to those whose roles involve some research and/or the creation and analysis of curriculum materials in the social studies or other curricular areas.

One cautionary suggestion: the materials in the Appendix are to be used in conjunction with Part Four, and should be consulted only *after* the "Exercises" in Chapter 8 are completed.

An important part of an author's ritual in completing a book is to attempt to acknowledge the innumerable contributions of others. This is, of course, an impossible task. The major intellectual debt to be credited here, however, is to the late Alan Griffin who greatly influenced my views on social-studies education, and who was largely responsible for stimulating my interest in cognitive processes.

Sincere thanks also go to those many youngsters in different classrooms across the United States who clarified, verified, and revised so much of my thinking concerning conceptual behavior. Particularly instructive were the eager students and the cooperative staff at the Sunset School in the Shoreline School District, Seattle, Washington, and in the Seattle Public Schools.

Research for portions of the book were supported through a much appreciated grant in aid from Temple University. The thankless but essential task of typing the entire manuscript was handled effortlessly and efficiently by Sheila Decaroli.

Special apologies are extended to my children who, when unfortunate enough to have peeked into their father's study during the past few years, were introduced to some very negative and often violent associations with "book." To my wife, Mary, whose strategically placed comment, "You have nothing to say—and you're belaboring the point," spared the reader much grief and nonsense, my deep and affectionate gratitude.

A concluding note of thanks is due to John Dugan and Roger Boulé at INTEXT for all their help, friendship, and patience during this project.

P.H.M.

Philadelphia, Pennsylvania
April, 1971

Contents

part *ONE*

Concept Learning in the Social-Studies Curriculum

CHAPTER 1

Concept Learning as an Objective

Educational institutions, like all others, must be responsive to their environment if they are to survive and grow. This basic axiom is now confronting American schools with a vengeance.

In their own way, teachers, students, parents, and citizens in general all share in an increasing thrust for more *relevance* in educational institutions, and all levels of schooling—preschool to graduate—have been shaken by this wave of involvement. Surprisingly, too, there is little in the substance of the cry against the dichotomy between the nature of the schools' activities and the nonschool world that is really new. Writing in 1916, for example, John Dewey warned:[1]

> There is the standing danger that the material of formal instruction will be merely the subject matter of the schools isolated from the subject matter of life-experience. The permanent social interests are likely to be lost from view. Those which have not been carried over into the structure of social life, but which remain largely matters of technical information expressed in symbols, are made conspicuous in schools. Thus we reach the ordinary notion of education: the notion which ignores its social necessity and its identity with all human association that affects conscious life, and which identifies it with imparting information about remote matters and the conveying of learning through verbal signs: the acquisition of literacy.

What *is* different about the contemporary scene is that our society as a whole appears to be more sensitive to the need for "relevance" and has better evaluative tools for establishing whether the test of relevance has been met. Groups within our society are now demanding, in increasing measure, that the schools be accountable both for their results and for their methods of ascertaining results. In short, the nature, mechanics, and conclusions of evaluation procedures are of increasing interest to the general society. We, as educators, are being strongly urged to demonstrate that the resources and objectives we employ—teachers, subject matter, materials, or procedures—are commensurate with the resources that society provides and that we are producing socially relevant results.

---

[1] John Dewey, *Democracy and Education* (New York: Macmillan, 1961), p. 8.

It is significant to note also that in recent years the most rapid changes in higher education have been initiated through student prodding rather than through traditional administrative mechanisms. Similarly, at lower levels, community pressures upon the elementary and secondary schools have opened the decision-making apparatus to a wider audience than teachers and administrators.

While the cry for relevance may be more of a waning shibboleth than a clear directive for change, the spirit of its message is clear to most educators who wish to listen. Amid a shifting mood of restlessness, often occasioned by violence, wanton destruction, and general irrationalism, many segments of our society are rejecting the traditional goals and corresponding means provided by our schools.

In a broader vein, the general goals and policies of government at all levels are being challenged by a diverse spectrum of groups, ranging from the traditional minority groups to the so-called "silent majority"—As they should be in a democratic society.

SOCIAL-STUDIES OBJECTIVES

Within the context of this climate of social concern over the direction of our society, the perennial controversy over educational objectives has taken on a new importance. This traditional issue is particularly significant and sensitive in the domain of the social studies, whose important goals, of necessity, must intersect with the pulse of social concerns.

Historically, social-studies educators have differed in their opinions concerning appropriate goals for the social studies. Edwin Fenton, for example, has indicated that "There are three popular conceptions of the purposes of social studies. Social studies prepare children to be good citizens; social studies teach children how to think; social studies pass on the cultural heritage."[2] Hunt and Metcalf, on the other hand, have argued that "The foremost aim of instruction in high school social studies is to help students reflectively examine issues in the problematic areas of American culture."[3]

In a succinct essay, *Alternative Directions for the Social Studies*,[4] Dale Brubaker has reflected the continuum of opinions within the profession on the issue of appropriate goals for the social studies. His suggestion, however, was that the spectrum of views may be bifurcated into two fundamental categories: supporters of "citizenship-education" objectives and supporters of "social-science-inquiry" objectives.[5] In the former group are the majority of social-studies educators, according to Brubaker.

Clearly, a variety of schema exist for categorizing objectives, and much of the

---

[2] Edwin Fenton, *The New Social Studies* (New York: Holt, 1967), p. 1.

[3] Maurice P. Hunt and Lawrence E. Metcalf, *Teaching High School Social Studies: Problems in Reflective Thinking and Social Understanding,* 2d ed. (New York: Harper, 1968), p. 288.

[4] Dale Brubaker, *Alternative Directions for the Social Studies* (Scranton, Pa.: International Textbook Co., 1967).

[5] *Ibid.,* Chapters 1 and 2.

contemporary reform movement within professional education circles is directed at the more precise specification of objectives. Regardless of social-studies educators' positions along an objective continuum or their general frames of reference concerning goals, *concept learning* is likely to be considered a highly desirable educational outcome. In this respect, *concept learning* as an educational focus allows educators to transcend, to some degree their global statement of goals.

In recent years, concept learning as an objective for the social studies has received considerable attention among social-studies educators.[6] "One of the functions of education and of school learning," Fancett and her associates have written, "is to transmit relatively definitive meanings of certain concepts, and at the same time transmit the ability to amend and revise concepts, as well as the ability to reorganize instances of experience into newly discovered or personally held concepts."[7] Reflecting this pattern, myriad curriculum materials have been advertised as being designed to teach significant social-science concepts. Similarly, at the classroom level, teachers have given some indications of sensing a need to force the subject matter of the social sciences into a conceptual framework for students.

This apparent consensus on the importance of concept learning is deceptive, however, as a careful analysis of the literature will reveal. Terminology is, at best, fuzzy, and definitions usually are absent or lack precision. In many respects, the term "concept" has become a catch-all category for cognitive operations and frequently is often used synonymously with "idea," "generalization," "structure," "topic," or "labels." Massialas observed this point in a 1962 report:[8]

> One could read several curriculum studies and social studies essays and texts and find as many different usages of the term "concept," a term which is fundamental to all learning and instruction in this particular area (social studies). In addition to this, many people refer to concepts on a very abstract level, with no effort, whatever, to provide some illustrative examples. It is often true that in committee meetings and lectures persons repeatedly use words such as "concepts," "ideas," "generalizations," "conclusions," and "hypotheses," but fail to suggest specific and relevant examples of each.

What the dialogue concerning concept learning has lacked, then, are common referents. Education in general, and social studies in particular, lacks a precise terminology through which practitioners could effectively communicate;

---

[6] See Hunt and Metcalf, *op. cit.;* Verna S. Fancett *et al. Social Science Concepts and the Classroom* (Syracuse, N.Y.: Social Studies Curriculum Center, 1968); Hilda Taba, *Teaching Strategies and Cognitive Functioning in Elementary School Children,* Cooperative Research Project No. 2404 (Washington, D.C: U.S. Office of Education, 1966); Marlin L. Tanck, "Teaching Concepts, Generalizations, and Constructs," *Social Studies Curriculum Development: Prospects and Problems, 39th Yearbook,* Dorothy McClure Fraser, ed. (Washington, D.C.: National Council for the Social Studies, 1969); and Edith West, "Concepts, Generalizations, and Theories: Background Paper #3," unpublished paper, Project Social Studies, University of Minnesota, no date.

[7] Fancett *et al., op. cit.,* p. 3.

[8] Byron G. Massialas, "Research Prospects in the Social Studies," *Indiana University School of Education Bulletin,* XXXVIII (January, 1962), 4.

progress in understanding the nature of concept learning has therefore suffered from this general malaise. Social-studies educator Alan Griffin sounded a warning in 1942,[9] that still has a contemporary ring, concerning "fuzzy and ungrounded verbalizing" which he saw as "one of the most serious handicaps now impeding the professionalization of education."

A second dimension of difficulty has stemmed from the failure of curriculum designers to match concept-learning objectives, however stated, with curricular materials. Little empirical or even logical evidence has been adduced to indicate, for example, that curricular materials labeled as "concept oriented" do, in fact, produce the outcomes specified. Furthermore, the arrangement of content (usually in chronological or topological fashion) within textbooks and related material bears, in most cases, little resemblance to that predicated by the general principles of concept learning reflected in the experimental literature. Since this matching of objectives, learning principles, subject-matter structure, and organization has not been made in most textual materials, subject matter must be "taken out of context" to make it contribute systematically to concept learning. Selakovich has made this point in the text, *Problems in Secondary Social Studies,* in a general commentary upon the failure of authors to use principles of learning theory in designing curricular materials.[10]

> Learning principles widely accepted in educational psychology have not yet been widely applied to curriculum organization and content in the social studies . . . the materials which constitute the social studies have yet to incorporate the ideas. Because social studies texts make little effort to organize content on the basis of principles of learning, such organization becomes the responsibility of the classroom teacher—and the extent to which learning principles are applied to teaching depends largely on the teacher's ability to apply them.

A final related problem associated with social-studies objectives concerns the failure of textual-material designers to recognize adequately the need for designing their products in structurally different ways for differing objectives. A variety of factors, many of them economic, account for this situation. The fact remains, however, that materials have been conventionally designed to achieve a range of objectives, explicit or implicit, with differing subject matter generally correlated in some narrative fashion with those objectives. The *structural* or *organizational* form of such subject matter, however, has generally been held *constant* across objectives. Thus, curricular materials for teaching "generalizations," for example, resemble structurally those used for teaching "concepts," even though the author may explicitly discriminate between the two categories of objectives. The erroneous impression implied by this state of affairs is that a

---

[9] Alan Griffin, "A Philosophical Approach to the Subject-Matter Preparation of Teachers of History," unpublished doctoral dissertation, The Ohio State University, 1942.
[10] Daniel Selakovich, *Problems in Secondary Social Studies* (Englewood Cliffs, N.J.: Prentice-Hall, 1965), p. 6.

single structural form for curricular materials is maximally efficient for effecting a variety of different types of cognitive learning.

THE SELECTION PROCESS IN CONCEPT LEARNING

Paradoxically, the associated products of the various social-studies projects across the United States since the early 1960's have both resolved and created problems for social-studies teachers. Not the least of the new problems is the issue of how the selection of subject matter from the wealth of materials available is to be made and how the various social-science disciplines are to be represented efficiently in the K-12 curriculum. Clearly, it is impossible to incorporate all the social sciences at all grade levels in the degree and scope recommended by project authors, even if this plan were deemed desirable. A focus upon concepts rather than disciplines or topics, however, provides at least some measure for selection of relevant subject matter. A key criterion of relevance in subject matter selection is the degree to which it has potential for teaching a concept, regardless of its discipline identification. The historian Edwin Saveth made a similar point:[11]

> Current efforts to cope with curricula, especially in the high schools, generally result in a tug of war between teachers of history and teachers of the social sciences themselves, as to how much of the subject matter of history and the disciplines is to be included. The premises of this argument are false once the concept is understood as being, by its nature, interdisciplinary and having a theoretical development in more than one social science. Much more could be accomplished if the social science teachers recognized that they were teaching concepts rather than disciplines and that the concept is illustrated best by concrete historical problems.

A note concerning an individual school's role in concept selection is now in order because considerable resources and talent have been consumed in recent years in seeking out definite lists of concepts that might be regarded as *the* concepts of particular disciplines. The serendipity fallout from such pursuits clearly has been useful in generating dialog among educators and social scientists, concerning social-studies education. Equally clear, however, is the fact that such searches have failed to achieve their originally stated objectives. While structural relationships obviously exist within disciplines and fundamental principles providing bases for the disciplines, the disciplines themselves provide no answers about essential concepts. Nor is such consensus essential for efficient curriculum development. It would seem prudent for educators to begin selecting, from the many important concepts already itemized in the literature, those important concepts that match the resources and constraints imposed by local school situations.

[11] Edward N. Saveth, "The Conceptualization of American History," *American History and the Social Sciences,* Edward N. Saveth, ed. (New York: Free Press, 1965), p. 16.

It is also likely that at least two variables not suggested directly by the social-science disciplines themselves will dictate the sequencing of the concepts selected: namely, the learning relationship of the concepts and the logical interrelationship of the concepts. In other words, does a given group of students have the prior learning experiences appropriate in learning a given new concept and is concept A logically subsumed under concept B.

Fancett and her associates have summarized the teacher's necessary concerns in this fashion:[12]

> Confronted with a body of knowledge that is to be taught, the teacher plans with that conceptual framework in mind, having asked himself:
> What concepts must the student know in order to deal with this concept?
> What added concepts are inherent in this content?
> If the student understands these concepts will he be able to relate important ideas and reach for important generalizations?
> What methods, techniques, materials will facilitate learning in this particular instance?

CONCEPT LEARNING AS INQUIRY

Those who have followed the course of social-studies education over the last decade are well aware that the topic of *inquiry* has dominated much of our methodological discussions. Inquiry in curricular settings has taken a variety of forms, but generally it has come to refer to instructional settings in which students are encouraged to volunteer or arrive at inferences and implications from observed subject matter. Deductive, inductive, or what has been called "seductive" procedures are used to generate such processes in students.

Virtually all social-studies materials that identify themselves with inquiry reflect either an explicit or implicit methodological model that bears at least a faint resemblance to John Dewey's notion of "reflective thinking." While an adequate discussion of his pertinent views are beyond the scope of this book,[13] the nexus between Dewey's notion of reflective thinking and concept learning may be seen in the conceptualization process inherent in reflective thinking. One engaged in reflective thought is necessarily categorizing, organizing, and relating observations into an overall pattern, as well as inferring and, eventually, verifying. Also consistent with Dewey's notions concerning the initiation of reflective thought, an act of concept learning may be seen as being triggered by the confrontation and delineation of puzzling, disturbing, curious, or problematical situations.

[12] Fancett *et al., op. cit.,* p. 44.
[13] For a discussion of the Dewey model applied to one dimension of classroom instruction in an analytic way, see James B. Kracht and Peter H. Martorella, "Simulation and Inquiry Models Applied to Environmental Problems," *Journal of Geography,* LXIX (May, 1970).

AN OVERVIEW

This book, then, will attempt to grapple with the issue of concept learning as applied to classroom instruction from a perspective that is narrower and more empirically based than existing, conventional accounts. Its basic assumption is that while much has been said concerning concept learning in the social studies and its importance, little has been organized in the way of systematic treatment of the issue.

Initial chapters will focus upon empirical investigations into concept learning as it occurs in classroom settings, how concepts have been perceived and analyzed by various investigators, and the conclusions that have been generated. These chapters will attempt to synthesize those significant observations of scholars in the field that have the greatest potential relevance for social-studies educators interested in devising more efficient concept-learning experiences.

Those findings will then be culled for guidelines concerning teaching, and the conclusions will be presented in subsequent chapters. The term "guidelines" is used advisedly because direct implications for specific subject areas are seldom apparent from general experimental research. Topics to be considered include the nature and parameters of concepts, the dimensions of concept learning, variables influencing concept learning, distinctions between concepts and generalizations, and instructional strategies.

Following these chapters, several different models for concept learning will be provided. These have been selected from a variety of sources in the literature and are intended to acquaint the reader with general schema for structuring concept learning at preschool, elementary, and secondary levels. As models, they are designed to have wide generalizability to disparate subject-matter areas, and to be of maximal value they should suggest to the reader a variety of specific applications tailored to meet the special requirements of his own classroom situation.

To facilitate application and to clarify these models further, Chapter 7 will include illustrations of each of the models as applied to social-studies instruction. These illustrations include conventional classroom techniques and also suggest newer approaches, such as computer-assisted instruction.

Subsequent chapters will offer exercises as preparation for concept learning and some suggested directions for curricular settings designed to promote concept learning. The exercises are designed to assist in developing a continuum of learning skills that will better prepare a student for concept learning. The suggestions for curricular settings include (1) specifications for organization of curricular materials such as books, films, and slides, (2) the organization and structural characteristics of instructional sequences, and (3) the discussion of individualization for both students and teachers. Finally, needed areas for research are indicated, and an analysis is made of the parameters of reform likely to be associated with shifting to a concept-oriented instructional program in the social studies.

SUGGESTED READINGS

Brubaker, Dale. *Alternative Directions for the Social Studies.* Scranton, Pa.: International Textbook Co., 1967.

A brief, basic categorization of the divergent views concerning the objectives of social studies teaching.

Dewey, John. *Democracy and Education.* New York: Macmillan, 1961.

Provides a design for the structuring of "relevant" social studies based upon bringing social and classroom concerns more in harmony.

Griffin, Alan. "A Philosophical Approach to the Subject-Matter Preparation of Teachers of History." Unpublished Ph.D. dissertation. Columbus: The Ohio State University, 1942.

One of the truly seminal pieces of social-studies education literature relating to rationale, objectives, and methodology.

Hunt, Maurice P., and Lawrence E. Metcalf. *Teaching High School Social Studies: Problems in Reflective Thinking and Social Understanding.* 2d ed. New York: Harper, 1968, Chap. 4.

An excellent, brief discussion of the distinctions between teaching facts, concepts, and generalizations in the social studies.

CHAPTER 2

Learning Concepts in Classrooms

A brief has been made for the case that considerable confusion exists concerning the nature of a concept. Furthermore, it has been demonstrated that the term is often used in quite different ways by various practitioners. A teacher, for example, may think of a concept as a learning objective for youngsters, whereas the philosopher may see a concept as an abstraction: And, still differently, the historian may regard a concept as an important building-block in the structure of his discipline.

All of the confusion concerning the nature of concepts and differing perceptions about the function of concepts necessarily is reflected in the research findings dealing with concept learning. While a considerable quantity of research on concepts has been amassed, unfortunately there is a serious question about how much of the findings may be applied to classroom instruction with any degree of assurance. Remstad has captured the essence of this issue in his statement:[1]

> An examination of the scores of experimental studies devoted to various aspects of concept learning leads to the conclusion that psychologists have compiled a considerable amount of information which should be relevant to the learning of the types of concepts taught in schools. However, closer examination raises the question whether or not that which the psychologist in his experimentation has labeled a concept bears an adequate enough resemblance to the type of concept taught in the classroom to be of value to educators.

This and subsequent chapters will focus on research into *how* organisms learn concepts, however defined by the experimenter, that may be relevant to classroom instruction. Only research that seemed to have applications to classroom instruction in the social studies was reviewed.

At least four basic levels of problems thread through attempts to survey the literature on concept learning:

---

[1] Robert C. Remstad, *Optimizing the Response to a Concept Attainment Test Through Sequential Classroom Experimentation,* Technical Report No. 85, Research and Development Center for Cognitive Learning (Madison: University of Wisconsin, 1969), p. 8.

1. Similar terminology is used with different specific meanings in various studies, although the general focus may be similar.
2. Different philosophical assumptions undergird otherwise similar studies.
3. Some studies focus on the learning of concepts under conditions similar to those which exist in the classroom, while others do not.
4. Some studies classify discriminations between the phases of concept learning, while others do not.

SEMANTICAL CONFUSION

What seems uncertain, as one surveys the field of concept literature, is whether the discussion is centered upon the learning of a common item. Platt, writing in *Social Education,* provides a useful observation on this point:[2]

> *What is a concept?* A simple answer would be, nobody knows; or rather, few are willing to advance a precise definition. Many, however, are willing to list some concepts without defining them. Mary Rusnak mentions "historical sequence," "cause and effect," and "geographical space" as concepts. Allan Nevins, the historian, refers to the United States as the producer of "new-world concept of independence," but he says nothing of the meaning of "concept."

Those who do attempt to reduce confusion and improve communications by defining their terms not infrequently disagree on the critical attributes of what they are discussing. A representative sampling of definitions from the literature is included below to suggest the differences of opinion that exist concerning the properties of concepts.

> A *concept* is a kind of unit in terms of which one thinks; a unit smaller than a judgment, proposition, or theory, but one which necessarily enters into these.[3]
>
> A concept in the most general sense is a schema for evaluating impinging stimulus objects or events.[4]
>
> In brief, concepts are properties of organismic experience—more particularly they are abstracted and often cognitively structured, classes of "mental" experience learned by organisms in the course of their life histories.[5]
>
> A concept may be thought of as "the common element shared by an array of objects" or "the relationship between the constituents or parts of a process."[6]

[2] Myles M. Platt, "Concepts and the Curriculum," *Social Education,* XXVII (January, 1963), 21.

[3] Julius Gould and William L. Kolb, eds., *A Dictionary of the Social Sciences* (New York: Free Press, 1964), p. 20.

[4] O. J. Harvey *et. al., Conceptual Systems and Personality Organization* (New York: Wiley, 1961), p. 10.

[5] John B. Carroll, "Words, Meanings and Concepts," *Harvard Educational Review,* XXIV (Spring, 1964), 180.

[6] F. H. George, *Cognition* (London: Methuen, 1962), p. 260.

Concepts are "particles," as it were, out of which all social behavior is formed.[7]

A concept is a generalized and abstract symbol; it is the sum total of all our knowledge of a particular class of objects . . . In short a concept is a condensation of experience.[8]

The basic concepts are essentially high level abstractions expressed in verbal cues and labels.[9]

A concept is a general idea, usually expressed by a word, which represents a class or group of things or actions having certain characteristics in common.[10]

A concept . . . is something about an idea expressed in the words of our language.[11]

In appraising the plethora of definitions available in the literature, the psychologist Vinacke has noted that "one of their greatest weaknesses is the unfortunate tendency to regard words as concepts rather than to recognize that a verbal response is merely a label for the internal cognitive system, which from the psychological standpoint, is actually the concept.[12]

The philosophical schools of thought concerning concepts were classified by Hullfish and Smith:[13]

(1) the concept has been considered to be an outright creation of an immaterial entity, the mind; (2) it has been viewed as a mental construct which emerges when a sensory quality common to many diverse mental objects is abstracted; and (3) it has been said to be, in effect, a covering response made to the quality common to numerous stimuli which are discrete on all other counts.

Yet, in another vein, the philosopher Gilbert Ryle has underscored the frequency with which psychological investigators have erred in assuming that an item *exists* because it has a name. He cautions that a lack of sensitivity for precision in terminology breeds erroneous conclusions about cognitive processes, and he suggests that much of the resulting experimental work has been fruitless because of just such a deficiency.[14]

If someone was under the impression that there did exist some such ingredient activities common and peculiar to gardening and working, he would be forced to allow that they were extremely difficult to isolate. I

[7] Edwin N. Saveth, "The Conceptualization of American History," *American History and the Social Sciences*, Edward N. Saveth, ed. (New York: Free Press, 1964), p. 16.

[8] Gaston Viaud, *Intelligence: Its Evolution and Form*, A. J. Pomerans, trans. (New York: Harper, 1960), pp. 75–76.

[9] Hilda Taba, "Techniques of In-Service Training," *Social Education*, XXIX (November, 1965), 465.

[10] Isaac J. Quillen and Lavone A. Hanna, *Education for Social Competence*, rev. ed. (Chicago: Scott Foresman, 1961), p. 187.

[11] Platt, *op. cit.*, p. 41.

[12] W. E. Vinacke, *The Psychology of Thinking* (New York: McGraw-Hill, 1952), p. 100.

[13] H. Gordon Hullfish and Philip G. Smith, *Reflective Thinking: The Method of Education* (New York: Dodd, 1961), pp. 152–153.

[14] Gilbert Ryle, "Thinking," *Acta Psychologica*, IX (1953), 192, 195.

suggest that part of the difficulty that the experimental psychologists have had in isolating any ingredient acts or states common and peculiar to thinking is just the same difficulty—that of isolating something which is not there to isolate . . . It is the search for some ingredients or mechanism, whether introspectible or unconscious, common and peculiar to all that goes by the name of "thinking" which seems to me to be a search for a will o' the wisp. My conclusion is that the experimental investigation of thinking has been, on the whole, unproductive, because the researchers have had confused or erroneous notions of what they were looking for. Their notions of what they were looking for were confused or erroneous partly because they were borrowed from the philosophical doctrines of the day. They were the heirs of conceptual disorders.

A similar warning was also raised by Hullfish and Smith:[15]

It appears that the search for *a concept* is fruitless. No such entity is to be discovered, despite the inspired efforts over the ages of students of "mental life" or those of the analyses of behavior. And research is ill conceived that investigates the formation and function of "a something" thought to be so well known that it need not be defined, with its existence taken for granted simply because there is a noun in the language that names it.

CLASSROOM VERSUS NONCLASSROOM CONCEPT LEARNING

The pattern that emerges from much of the psychological research on concept learning since the 1920's is generally consistent. The emphasis has been on studying both the attributes that are critical to the concepts in question and the information-handling task required of the subject. Usually taken into account is the sequence in which the positive and negative examples are introduced to the subject and the amount of information about the concept that is provided. Generally, throughout most of the experiments, the procedure has been centered primarily around the following task, as Carroll has observed:[16]

The subject is presented with a series of instances which are differentiated in some way: either the task is finding out in what way the several instances match up with one of a small number of names, or (in the simpler case) it is one of discovering why some instances are "positive" (*i.e.,* instances of the concept the experimenter has in mind) or "negative" (not instances of the "concept"). Typically the stimulus material consists of a simple visual material characterized by a number of clearly salient dimensions—*e.g.,* the color of the figures, the geometrical shape of the figures, the number of figures, the number of boarders, the color of the background, etc.

As the reader may have surmised already, what hampers the generalizability of these laboratory studies is their questionable relationship to concepts commonly

---

[15] Hullfish and Smith, *op. cit.,* p. 160.
[16] Carroll, *op. cit.,* p. 198.

learned in one's life experiences and the context in which they are normally learned. Bruner has cautioned,[17] "Learning theory, for example, is distilled from descriptions of behavior in situations where the environment has been arranged either for the convenience of observing learning behavior or out of a theoretical interest in some special aspect of learning-reinforcement, cue distinctiveness or whatnot." While scientific rigor and efficiency may dictate the desirability of isolating variables to the point of constructing artificial concepts, the obvious question of the utility and relevance of such experimentation for practical, pursuits in the classroom remains unanswered. It would seem fair to say that it is precisely the experimentally desirable relative objectivity of the laboratory concepts that casts doubts for many educators upon the transfer value of the experimenters' conclusions.

Carroll's observation is pertinent, here:[18] "It is not self-evident that there is any continuity at all between learning 'DAX' as the name of a certain geometrical shape of a certain color and learning the meaning of the term 'longitude.'" Some of the more significant differences between concepts learned in the laboratory under controlled conditions and those concepts usually learned under normal classroom conditions have been summarized by Carroll;[19] the gist of the distinction follows:

1. A new concept which is learned in school is usually a genuinely new concept rather than an artificial combination of known properties.
2. In the classroom, new concepts learned depend upon properties which themselves also represent difficult concepts.
3. Many difficult school concepts are of the *relational variety* concerning which little has been revealed from experimental data.
4. An important problem in school learning is remembering many words and concepts, many of which are often dissimilar.
5. The most significant difference between concept learning in the classroom and the learning of concepts in the laboratory is that the former is chiefly deductive and the latter is generally inductive.

Remstad indicated two other important differences between the two types of learning conditions:[20] (1) a student must learn a new word or a new use for a known word along with the concept; and (2) neither the exemplars of the concept nor the dimensions to be considered can be listed or can be observed completely, so that "an unambiguous or complete attainment of a concept is impossible."

[17] Jerome S. Bruner, "Education as Social Invention," *Journal of Social Issues*, XX (July, 1964), 32.
[18] Carroll, *op. cit.*, pp. 179–180.
[19] *Ibid.*, pp. 190–191.
[20] Remstad, *op. cit.*, p. 12.

CLASSIFYING DISCRIMINATIONS

The literature contains several classification models for distinguishing types of concepts. While some of the schema are primarily attempts to inject operational definitions into terms heretofore loosely used, others try to distinguish between the active and passive phases of a concept or to label the distinctions involved in teaching and learning a concept. Still others are concerned with discriminating between varieties of concepts.

Klausmeier and his associates, for example, speak of a "categorizing-type" concept:[21]

> One type of concept is the inferences that one has formed of objects or events that enable one to categorize them as belonging to the same class and to associate the relevant observable and unobservable class attributes to them and to other members of the same class. Some functions of concepts of the categorizing type are generally acknowledged. Possessing a concept enables the individual to categorize objects and events as belonging to the same class or not belonging to it; in turn, this renders the environment less complex. Furthermore, by possessing certain concepts, the individual can identify more readily new objects as he encounters them.

In many respects both their constructs and the thrust of their arguments closely resemble those of Bruner *et al.* in *A Study of Thinking*. In this work, Bruner and his associates establish three distinct classes of concepts: conjunctive, disjunctive, and relational. They consider each class to relate to a different mode of coupling attributes.[22]

A *conjunctive* concept is defined in terms of a common class of combined elements; an example would be "island"—"a body of land surrounded on all sides by water." *Disjunctive* concepts, on the other hand, take their identity from the fact that they have *alternate* attributes. An instance of a disjunctive concept, Bruner *et al.* tell us, is a strike in baseball. Since a strike may be a pitched ball resulting in any one of several different phenomena, its category identity is preserved even though its attributes may vary at any given moment. The third class, *relational* concepts, express a certain relationship among the attributes of a concept. An example might be the class of income-tax brackets which the government establishes and defines in terms of the relational properties between one's income and the number of dependents he has.

Bruner *et al.* also see relationships among these three schema within the context of their further classification distinction: concept formation and concept attainment.[23]

---

[21] Herbert J. Klausmeier *et. al., Strategies of Learning and Efficiency of Concept Attainment by Individuals and Groups,* Cooperative Research Project (Washington, D. C.: U.S. Office of Education, 1964), p. 2.

[22] Jerome S. Bruner, Jacqueline J. Goodnow, and George Austin, *A Study of Thinking* (New York: Science Editions, 1962), p. 41.

[23] *Ibid.,* p. 45.

Hullfish, H. Gordon, and Phillip G. Smith. *Reflective Thinking: The Method of Education.* New York: Dodd, Mead, 1961, Chap. 10.

A well-written and succinct analysis of conceptualizing as a process and its implications for classroom instruction.

Hunt, Maurice P., and Lawrence E. Metcalf. *Teaching High School Social Studies: Problems in Reflective Thinking and Social Understanding,* 2d ed. New York: Harper, 1968, Chap. 4.

An excellent, brief discussion of the distinctions between teaching facts, concepts, and generalizations in the social studies.

part TWO

Research on Concept Learning: Findings, Issues, and Applications

CHAPTER 3

Research on Concept Learning in Laboratories and Classrooms

CONCEPT LEARNING IN THE LABORATORY

One of the more important hallmark studies of concept learning, *A Study of Thinking* by Jerome Bruner and his associates, was published in 1956.[1] This book reported on twenty laboratory experiments on concept attainment in which the following procedure was used. Subjects are presented with a board containing a number of objects. Each object has a set of dimensions with corresponding values. Subjects are informed that the items can be divided into two mutually exclusive groups with membership defined by a rule (concept) consisting of certain attributes. An object is designated as a member of the group, and from this the subjects are to discover the classification rule by selecting objects and then having the experimenter designate their group membership. The subject is to reveal the classification rule as soon as he recognizes it, at which time the concept is considered attained.

Since these studies have possibly had a greater influence upon concept-learning research than any other, an extensive summary of them seems in order. The experiments generated considerable data concerning (1) the distinction between concept formation and attainment, (2) the different types of concepts that exist, (3) a working definition of a concept, and (4) the learning set that one has for a concept-learning task.

Concept Formation and Attainment. Concept or category formation in these studies refers to the act by which classes are constructed, whereas concept attainment is the process of learning what features of the environment are relevant for grouping events into externally defined classes. Concept attainment is the search for and testing of attributes that can be used to distinguish exemplars from

[1] Jerome S. Bruner, Jacqueline J. Goodnow, and George Austin, *A Study of Thinking* (New York: Science Editions, 1962), p. 33.

nonexemplars of various categories.[2] Bruner *et al*. provide a list of the decisions involved in attaining a concept.

1.1. *The definition of the task*. What does the person take as the objective of his behavior? What does he think he is supposed to do?

1.2. *The nature of the instances encountered*. How many attributes does each exhibit, and how many of these are defining and how many noisy? Does he encounter instances at random, in a systematic order, and does he have any control over the order in which instances will be tested? Do instances encountered contain sufficient information for learning the concept fully?

1.3. *The nature of validation*. Does the person learn each time an instance is encountered whether it is or is not an exemplar of the concept whose definition he is seeking? Or is such validation only available after a series of encounters? Can hypotheses be readily checked or not?

1.4. *The consequences of specific categorizations*. What is the price of categorizing a specific instance wrongly and the gain from a correct categorization? What is the price attached to a wrong hypothesis? And do the various contingencies—rightness or wrongness of a categorization of "X" and "not-X"—have a different price attached to them?

1.5. *The nature of imposed restrictions*. Is it possible to keep a record of instances and contingencies? Is there a price attached to the testing of instances as a means of finding out in which category they belong? Is there pressure of time to contend with, a need for speedy decisions?

Types of Concepts. As noted earlier, three types of concepts (conjunctive, disjunctive, and relational) were inferred. It was found that subjects tended to prefer *common-element* or conjunctive concepts over the other types. Part of the process of attaining disjunctive and relational concepts appears to be confounded by the set that a subject has developed in attaining conjunctive concepts. Whether this phenomenon "is a universal characteristic of human thought and language of Western cultures," the authors are not prepared to say.[3]

Working Definition of a Concept. Based upon abstracting a description of the processes at work in concept attainment, Bruner *et al*. define concept in the following terms:[4]

We have found it more meaningful to regard a concept as a network of significant inferences by which one goes beyond a set of *observed* critical properties exhibited by an object or event to the class identity of the object or event in question, and thence to additional inferences about other *unobserved* properties of the object or event. We see an object that is red, shiny, and roundish, and infer that it is an apple; we are then enabled to infer

[2] *Ibid*., p. 33.
[3] *Ibid*., p. 238.
[4] *Ibid*., p. 244.

further that "if it is an apple, it is also edible, juicy, will rot if left unrefrig-erated, etc." The working definition of a concept is the network of inferences that are or may be set into play by an act of categorization.

In general, it may be said that a *concept* minimally involves the process wherein an individual is confronted with the task of identifying and placing events into classes based on the principle of using certain critical characteristics and ignoring others.[5]

Learning Frame of Reference. A final set of conclusions from the studies relates to the issue of the learner's psychological frame of reference in confronting a concept-attainment task.[6]

> One other matter of technique has to do with the use of indirect or "cover-story" methods of studying cognition, a matter that has bedeviled the field of concept attainment particularly. If one presents a concept-attain-ment task to subjects with the cover-story instruction that it is a task of rote memory (associating DAXes and CIVs with various curlecues), then the behavior of the subject will be geared to the objectives of the task as stated and his strategy will reflect the requirements set him. Let it be clear that the problem of setting the objectives in problem-solving and conceptualizing experiments is not a nuisance to be got rid of by "cute" instructions that conceal the purpose of the research. Objective-setting is a critical variable to be studied as a variable; it is neither a parameter one can hold constant with safety nor an embarrassment to be swept under the procedural rug.

Related Studies

The influence of *A Study of Thinking* upon concept research has been con-siderable, and a number of related studies have appeared in the past fourteen years.[7] A study by Bourne,[8] for example, supported the conclusions of Bruner *et al.* concerning the factors that affect strategies used in concept-learning tasks.

Another such related study dealt with the development of a computer model of the attainment process.[9] Its objective was to develop a model of the various cognitive processes involved in human concept attainment and then provide a corresponding computer program to serve as a vehicle. Unlike other computer-cognitive simulation studies, the author built upon the construct of what he

[5] *Ibid.,* p. 232.

[6] *Ibid.,* p. 243.

[7] Curiously, there appears to be little transference of the conclusions of this study to the social-studies project, "Man—A Course of Study," with which Bruner himself has been directly associated.

[8] Lyle E. Bourne, Jr., "Factors Affecting Strategies Used in Problems of Concept-Forma-tion," *American Journal of Psychology,* LXXVI (1963), 229–238. See also the more recent collection of studies by Bruner and associates, *Studies in Cognitive Growth* (New York: Wiley, 1966).

[9] Frank B. Baker, *The Development of a Computer Model of the Concept Attainment Process: A Final Report.* Theoretical Paper No. 16, Research and Development Center for Cognitive Learning (Madison: University of Wisconsin, 1968).

refers to as "process psychology."[10] Additionally, he makes a distinction in his model between internal and external information in processing data for concept attainment:[11]

> The majority of information processed does not come from the external world but is created internally by the subject. Thus, although concept attainment is an information-processing problem, the amount of external information processed [is] minimal and consists only of the objects, the experimenter's instructions, and his designation of object choices or of concepts . . . As the majority of information is created internally, it is the task of psychologists to determine what internal information is created and how it is processed. . . . If one is to develop an adequate computer model, one must know what information is created, on what basis a subject created the information, what he did with it, and how much of it was retained for longer term use. Without substantial knowledge of this type it becomes difficult to develop sophisticated computer models. Unfortunately the current techniques of psychological experimentation do not seem capable of providing the requisite insight.

Examining a different dimension of concept learning—the effects of various types of different presentations—Kates and Yudin concluded that the presentation of all exemplars simultaneously was an optimal sequence strategy for concept learning.[12] In their study, students were given *successive presentations* in which examples were shown briefly and then removed, *focus conditions* sequences, in which two exemplars were always shown (a positive exemplar plus a new one— either positive or negative), and *simultaneous presentations,* wherein every new exemplar was shown *together with* all the previous exemplars. Their findings indicated a superiority hierarchy of *simultaneous presentations* to *focus condition* to *successive presentation.*

While the research findings concerning the ratios and the orders of positive and negative exemplars in concept-learning tasks have been inconclusive,[13] Bourne and Guy, in a 1968 report, suggest some important variables for consideration.[14] From their study with laboratory-type concepts, they concluded that both the concept rule and the nature of the learning problem must be taken into account as affecting the role of positive and negative exemplars.[15] This conclusion represents a qualification of Glaser's generalization, "As the information required

---

[10] *Ibid.*, p. 1.

[11] *Ibid.*, p. 36.

[12] Solis L. Kates and Lee Yudin, "Concept Attainment and Memory," *Journal of Educational Psychology,* LV (1964), 103–109.

[13] For a recent review of the research, see Joe L. Byers, "Verbal and Concept Learning," *Review of Educational Research,* XXXVII (1967), 494–513.

[14] Lyle E. Bourne, Jr., and Donald E. Guy, "Learning Conceptual Rules II: The Role of Positive and Negative Instances," *Journal of Experimental Psychology,* LXXVII (1968), 488–494.

[15] *Ibid.*, p. 494.

to define the concept is increasingly carried by negative rather than positive instances, concept learning becomes increasingly difficult."[16]

One of the early studies to examine the effects of irrelevant information in nonconjunctive concept learning was conducted by Kepros and Bourne.[17] Haygood and Stevenson,[18] in extending this study, concluded that the effects of adding irrelevant stimulus information with nonconjunctive rules[19] paralleled those for conjunctive concepts—a linear decrease in performance results. The actual rate of decrease, they concluded, was highly dependent upon the specific characteristics of the conceptual problem.

CONCEPT LEARNING IN THE CLASSROOM

While Bruner and his associates have generated a number of hypotheses and additional research studies concerning the learning of artificial concepts in laboratory settings, the scope of related research with "classroom" concepts in "clasroom" settings is considerably narrower. Sax, in a recent review of the research literature, has noted; for example, that:[20]

> From the period 1960 to the present, there has been an almost complete lack of research interest in concept information in areas other than mathematics and science. . . . Generally, the published material on concept formation in the social studies . . . has tended to be vague or weak in experimental design or has included suggestions for innovations without evidence to support them.

Two major researchers who have written and worked extensively in areas relating to classroom concepts learning are David Ausubel and Robert Gagné. Both have had considerable influence upon other researchers, the shaping of curriculum, and the analysis of learning conditions in naturalistic settings.

In his recent book, *Educational Psychology: A Cognitive View,* Ausubel has drawn upon his own research and others to draw some general conclusions concerning concept learning:[21]

---

[16] Robert Glaser, "Concept Learning and Concept Teaching," *Learning Research and School Subjects,* Robert M. Gagné and William J. Gephart, eds. (Itasca, Ill. Peacock, 1968), p. 15.

[17] P. G. Kepros and Lyle E. Bourne, Jr., "Identification of Bioconditional Concepts. Effects of the Number of Relevant and Irrelevant Dimensions," *Canadian Journal of Psychology,* XX (1966), 198–207.

[18] R. C. Haygood and M. Stevenson, "Effects of Number of Irrelevant Dimensions in Conjunctive Concept Learning," *Journal of Experimental Psychology,* LXXIV (1967), 302–304.

[19] Their nonconjunctive concepts are labeled "inclusive disjunction" (either red *or* square *or* both) and "conditional" (if red, *then* square).

[20] Gilbert Sax, "Concept Formation," *Encyclopedia of Educational Research,* 4th ed. Robert L. Ebel, ed. (New York: Macmillan, 1969), p. 201.

[21] David P. Ausubel, *Educational Psychology: A Cognitive View* (New York: Holt, 1968), pp. 526–527.

Thus concepts and propositions are typically acquired during the post-infancy, preschool, and early elementary-school years as a result of inductive processing of verbal and nonverbal concrete–empirical experience—typically through autonomous problem solving or discovery. The young child, for example, acquired the concept of a chair by abstracting the common features of the concept from multiple incidental encounters with many different sizes, shapes, and colors of chairs and then generalizing these attributes. Reception learning, on the other hand, although occurring early, does not become a prominent feature of intellectual functioning until the child becomes sufficiently mature cognitively to comprehend verbally presented concepts and propositions in the absence of concrete, empirical experience (until he can comprehend, for example, the meaning of "democracy" or "acceleration" from their dictionary definitions. In other words, inductive concept *formation* based on nonverbal concrete, empirical problem-solving experience exemplified early developmental phases of information processing, whereas simple concept *assimilation* through meaningful verbal reception learning exemplifies later stages.

Gagné's analysis of his own and other research on learning has led him to postulate the existence of *eight* types of learning conditions in a hierarchical arrangement, of which *concept* learning is type 6.[22]

Problem-Solving (type 8) requires as prerequisites
Principle (type 7) which requires as prerequisites
Concepts (type 6) which require as prerequisites
Multiple Discriminations (type 5) which require as prerequisites
Verbal Associations (type 4) or other chains (type 3) which require as prerequisites
Stimulus-Response Connections (type 2)
Signal Learning (type 1) is *not* considered a prerequisite to the other types of learning.

Concept learning is explained by Gagné as a way of putting things into a class and responding to the class as a whole.[23] He notes further that one must know a concept by reference to a class of concrete situations.[24] In essence, then, his definition is similar to that cited by Bruner *et al.* For Gagné the test for the presence of a concept is whether an organism can demonstrate that generalizing can occur:

There must be a demonstration that the learner can generalize the concept to a variety of specific instances of the class that have not been used in learning. Otherwise, it is not a concept, but merely a collection of specified chains.[25]

According to Gagné an instructional sequence designed to teach a concept—for example, edge—might proceed as follows:[26]

---

[22] Robert M. Gagné, *The Conditions of Learning* (New York: Holt, 1965), p. 60.
[23] *Ibid.,* p. 126.
[24] *Ibid.,* p. 132.
[25] *Ibid.,* p. 136.
[26] *Ibid.,* pp. 134–135.

(a) Show the child one instance of the concept (*e.g.*, edge, as the edge edge of a piece of paper), and say "This is an edge."

(b) Show him another instance, such as the edge of a swimming pool, and say, "This is not an edge."

(c) Show him a negative instance, such as the side or top of a cylinder, and say, "This is not an edge."

(d) Show him still another object, such as a cup, and pointing appropriately, say, "This is an edge," and "This is not an edge."

(e) A a test, give the child a box and say, "Show me the edge."

Applying Laboratory Research

Two recent studies by Remstad and by Frayer and Klausmeier investigated the extent to which conclusions generated by laboratory studies concerning concept learning could be generalized to classroom conditions.

Remstad specifically measured the effects of research-oriented mathematics instruction through slide-tape presentations upon the learning of selected concepts—"quadrilateral," "isosceles triangle," "trapezoid," and "rectangle." Eight variables were examined:[27]

(1) amount of redundant information;
(2) mode of presentation of successive instances;
(3) ratio of positive and negative instances;
(4) order of positive and negative instances;
(5) amount of information in accompanying verbal cues;
(6) length of time the instances are available to students;
(7) length of time between instances; and
(8) relative complexity of concept.

Among his conclusions were the findings that classroom instruction based upon principles of concept learning derived from laboratory studies *did* facilitate the learning of concepts and that verbal cues and time increments were significant variables.

Frayer and Klausmeier similarly examined, through the medium of *printed instructional materials*, the effects of emphasizing relevant attribute values and varying the number of examples on the learning of the mathematical concepts— "quadrilateral," "kite," "trapezoid," "parallelogram," "rectangle," "rhombus," and "square."[28] As with the Remstad study, upper-elementary students in classroom settings were the experimental subjects. Each of the concepts were analyzed to determine their relevant and irrelevant attributes, their rules, appropriate

---

[27] Robert C. Remstad, *Optimizing the Response to a Concept Attainment Test Through Sequential Classroom Experimentation*, Technical Report No. 85, Research and Development Center for Cognitive Learning (Madison: University of Wisconsin, 1969), p. ix–x.

[28] Dorothy A. Frayer and Herbert J. Klausmeier, "Effects of Instructional Variations on Mastery of Geometric Concepts by Fourth- and Sixth-Grade Children," paper presented at the annual meeting of the *American Educational Research Association*, March 2–6, 1970, Minneapolis, Minnesota.

exemplars and nonexemplars, and related subordinate and supraordinate concepts. Results of the study indicated "that variables found effective in laboratory concept learning may facilitate learning from printed instructional material.'[29]

Research in Social Studies

While these studies were carefully controlled and conducted in classroom settings, generalizing their conclusions to social-studies instruction must be approached cautiously. One reason is as Taba, Levine, and Elzey warn:[30]

> There is considerable reason to be concerned about the fact that the current research and curriculum experimentation are concentrated largely in the fields of science and mathematics. The models of thought emerging from these studies are likely to bear an imprint of the kind of thinking appropriate to these disciplines. The question is whether the models and processes of thought which are appropriate to science and mathematics are equally appropriate to areas such as the social studies and literature. There is substantial evidence to the effect that each subject field has its own distinct structure, in the sense of involving a distinct set of concepts, a distinct way of asking questions about the world, requiring different levels of precision, and distinct approaches to solving problems.

A related consideration to be weighed before generalizing findings from other subject-matter areas to the social studies, is the characteristics of social-science concepts. Often, even with basic social-science concepts, it is difficult to accomplish precise rule specification, attribute delineation, and exemplar construction, and accurate model referrents are hard to come by. Seemingly basic concepts, such as "river" and "army," present a variety of instructional difficulties if the tasks are analyzed carefully in terms of rules, criterial attributes, exemplars, and nonexemplars. The classroom models available for these two concepts do *not* reveal all of the attributes necessary to define the concepts. Additionally, it may be argued that many if not most of the social-science concepts usually investigated in classrooms are of the *nonconjunctive* variety, for which little empirical research data, from any subject area, exists.

Several studies, dealing with various aspects of concept learning, have worked directly with social-science concepts in classroom-related settings. Using the concepts of "lobbying" and "subsidizing," Grannis made a study of sixth-grade students who were presented with case-study exemplars to learn those concepts.[31] The effects of additional information (learning exercises) and a requirement to write a definition of the concept were analyzed. While the

29 *Ibid.*, p. 16.

30 Hilda Taba, Samuel Levine, and Freeman Elzey, *Thinking in Elementary School Children*. Cooperative Research Project No. 1574 (Washington, D.C.: U.S. Office of Education, 1964), p. 26.

31 Joseph C. Grannis, "An Experimental Study of the Inductive Learning of Abstract Social Concepts," unpublished doctoral dissertation, Washington University, St. Louis, 1965.

author did not find that these were significant variables, approximately 15 percent of the students were able to demonstrate mastery in recognizing new cases as positive or negative instances of the concept and to correctly change such instances from positive to negative or vice versa.

Concerned with different variables, Newton and Hickey examined the effects of prior instruction and the learning of subconcepts upon the learning rate of the concept "gross national product."[32] Their conclusion was that performance was faster when the advance information was given first and when the subconcepts of "consumption" and "investment spending" were learned together rather than discretely.

A comparison of alternative strategies for teaching concepts was analyzed by Nuthall in a study involving 432 tenth- and eleventh-grade students.[33] Four operationally discrete strategies were used to teach the concepts of "cultural symbosis" and "ethnocentrism" through the medium of programmed-text materials. Six statements for each of the two concepts determined their parameters for the teaching strategies. Other variables examined were the students level of knowledge related to the concepts and the content of instruction immediately preceding the strategies. Nuthall found that differences in teaching strategy (as defined in the study) could be related to differences in student performance on open-ended and multiple-choice criterion tests used in the study.

PIAGET'S RESEARCH

The work of Piaget[34] and his Geneva associates represents one strain of the small number of forces which have had a profound effect upon American educators in recent years. Although none of his research has been conducted in normal classroom settings, nor aimed toward such, it bears our examination here because it involved young children in concept-learning activities. The learning tasks given or assumed by children were "real life" experiences in the sense that they might normally be found in classrooms or in everyday activities.

Among other conclusions, the Piaget studies suggest that the attainment

[32] John M. Newton and Albert E. Hickey, "Sequence Effects in Programmed Learning of a Verbal Concept," *Journal of Educational Psychology*, LVI (1965), 140–147.

[33] Graham Nuthall, "An Experimental Comparison of Alternative Strategies for Teaching Concepts," *American Educational Research Journal*, V (1968), 561–584.

[34] See, for example: J. Piaget, *The Child's Conception of Physical Causality* (London: Routledge and Kegan Paul, 1930); *The Child's Conception of the World* (London: Routledge and Kegan Paul, 1951); *Judgment and Reason in the Child* (New York: Harcourt, 1929); *The Language and Thought of the Child* (New York: Harcourt, 1926); *The Moral Judgment of the Child* (New York: Macmillan, 1965); *The Origin of Intelligence in Children* (New York: International University Press, 1952); *The Psychology of Intelligence* (London: Routledge and Kegan Paul, 1950); and J. Piaget and B. Inhelder, *The Growth of Logical Thinking from Childhood to Adolescence* (New York: Basic Books, 1958).

of such concepts as time, weight, color, and distance occur developmentally as a youngster ages. More specifically, their findings have generated a general schema providing, in Hooper's terms, the *"right kind* of experience at the *right time* for the developing organism,"[35] thus suggesting what type of data is appropriate for learning at a given stage and how it should be presented.

Basic to any discussion of Piaget's findings relevant to concept learning, are his concepts of "accommodation," "assimilation," "stages," and "equilibrium." A summary of their meanings follows:

Accommodation. When an individual encounters new circumstances where his sensorimotor organization does not fit, that modification process or reorganization that takes place within his psychological structure may be considered as accommodation.

Assimilation. The process of internalizing or incorporating the accommodative change may be considered as assimilation. These two complementary processes, then, are simultaneously present in every act, and together they form the process of *adaptation.* Ginsburg and Opper offer an illustration of how these processes may appear and interrelate:[36]

> Consider an example of adaptation in infancy. Suppose an infant of 4 months is presented with a rattle. He has never before had the opportunity to play with rattles or similar toys. The rattle, then is a feature of the environment to which he needs to adapt. His subsequent behavior reveals the tendencies of assimilation and accommodation. The infant tries to grasp the rattle. In order to do this successfully he must accommodate in more ways than are immediately apparent. First, he must accommodate his visual activities to perceive the rattle correctly; then he must reach out and accommodate his movements to the distance between himself and the rattle; in grasping the rattle he must adjust his fingers to its shape; and in lifting the rattle he must accommodate his muscular exertion to its weight. In sum, the grasping of the rattle involves a series of acts of accommodation, or modifications of the infant's behavioral structures to suit the demands of the environment.

Stage. Stage refers to a pattern of behavior that appears to characterize some definable period in an individual's life. Piaget's findings indicate four major periods in the intellectual development of an individual: sensorimotor (birth to eighteen months); preoperational (eighteen months to seven years); concrete operational (seven years to eleven years); and formal operational (eleven years and over). During the *sensorimotor* period the child passes through six successive stages and moves from being centered about the self to conceiving of objects independent of him and of his self-identity and to gradually coordinating his motor activities and perceptions. For Piaget, the ordering of the stages is

---

[35] Frank H. Hooper, "Piagetian Research and Education," *Logical Thinking in Children,* Irving E. Sigel and Frank H. Hooper, eds. (New York: Holt, 1968), p. 423.

[36] Herbert Ginsburg and Sylvia Opper, *Piaget's Theory of Intellectual Development: An Introduction* (Englewood Cliffs, N.J.: Prentice-Hall, 1969), p. 19.

invariant; a child must pass through stage one before stage two and may not skip steps.

Equilibrium. The notion of equilibrium refers to a state of harmony between elements that have been in disequilibrium. It involves compatibility with one's environment and an organism psychologically at rest. Of the concept and its relationship to the child, Ginsburg and Opper write:[37]

> Throughout development the child moves from states of a lesser to those of a greater degree of equilibrium. The tendency toward equilibrium results in an increase in coherence and stability; this stability is acquired by activity on the part of the child. The child is active in the sense that he compensates for changes in the world, either by means of overt actions, as in the sensori-motor period, or by internal mental operations, as in the older child. With age the equilibrium becomes more stable because the child can anticipate changes and compensate in advance.

Piaget and Structure

Much of the contemporary discussion concerning *structure* has been associated with Piaget, perhaps because of his frequent allusions to "mental structure." His position on the topic, however, bears faint resemblance to the notion implicit in many so-called "structure-based" curricula in which students are taught the unifying themes of a subject area. His statement makes his position on the matter clear:[38]

> The question comes up whether to teach the structure, or to present the child with situations where he is active and creates the structures himself. The goal in education is not to increase the amount of knowledge, but to create the possibilities for a child to invent and discover. When we teach too fast, we keep the child from inventing and discovering himself . . . Teaching means creating situations where structures can be discovered; it does not mean transmitting structures which may be assimilated at nothing other than a verbal level.

Piaget's point is not that intellectual development proceeds at its own pace regardless of the teacher's efforts, but rather that what usually is attempted in schools is ineffective—"You cannot further understanding in a child simply by talking to him."[39]

The extent to which Piaget's theories differ from those of such contemporary American psychologists as Gagné and Skinner has been sketched by Flavell and Wohlwill:[40]

---

[37] *Ibid.,* p. 174.

[38] Quoted in Eleanor Duckworth, "Piaget Rediscovered," *Piaget Rediscovered,* Richard E. Ripple and Verne N. Rockcastle, eds. Cooperative Research Project No. F-040 (Washington, D.C.: U.S. Office of Education, 1964), p. 3.

[39] *Ibid.,* p. 2.

[40] John H. Flavell and Joachim F. Wohlwill, "Formal and Functional Aspects of Cognitive Development, *Studies in Cognitive Development: Essays in Honor of Jean Piaget,* David Elkind and John H. Flavell, eds. (New York: Oxford University Press, 1969), p. 109.

For psychologists such as Gagné and more particularly those operating from within a Skinnerian framework, it seems that the problem of the child's "readiness to learn" can in fact be reduced to the question of whether he has mastered all of the steps in the sequence that precede and are prerequisites for the concept to be learned. This assumption appears to ignore the problem of horizontal transfer, i.e., the interrelationships among cognitive structures that are coordinate as to level.

They suggest that Gagné's position in particular differs from Piaget's emphasis on structurally interrelated concepts forming a stage.

Piagetian Findings and the Social Studies

Although most of the direct applications to classroom subjects of Piaget's research are in the areas of science and math, E. A. Peel has speculated about the implications for social studies and the problems inherent in transferral of Piaget's ideas.[41] He notes that, unlike science, the data of history, for example, consists essentially of the intentions behind the actions of people in the past.[42]

> The first bridge, therefore, the teacher of history has to cross is that between present and past. He accounts for the past by whatever knowledge he can use from the child's present experience and by whatever concrete historical material he has available. In this way he builds up the right historical data. . . . But there is more to history than this. Its course can be viewed as a series of equilibria and disequilibria between the acts and intentions of men. The mature student of history is sensitive to the fine interplays and balance in such situations as the events in 1939 leading up to the Second World War . . .
>
> The balance of powers, physical or human, involves the two important principles of cancellation and compensation which forms an essential part of Piaget's account of adolescent thinking. Some investigations carried out recently using short passages of history demonstrated that this sensitivity is under present educational circumstances, a characteristic of mid-adolescence.

A second equation between Piagetian ideas and social-studies curriculum has been developed by Frank Hooper. He indicates a correspondence among (1) probabilistic reasoning, (2) multiple classification, (3) multiple causation, and (4) conservation of invariants and social-studies teaching, as the outline on top of page 35 indicates.[43]

Irving Sigel also related Piagetian findings to social-studies teaching through a series of illustrations dealing with the American Revolution. Initially, he addresses himself to the task of classification:[44]

---

[41] E. A. Peel, "Learning and Thinking in the School Situation," *Piaget Rediscovered,* Richard E. Ripple and Verne N. Rockcastle, eds. Cooperative Research Project No. F-040 (Washington, D.C.: U. S. Office of Education, 1964), pp. 103–104.

[42] *Ibid.*

[43] Hooper, *op. cit.,* pp. 426–429.

[44] Irving E. Sigel, *Child Development and Social Science Education: A Teaching Strategy Derived from Some Piagetian Concepts, Part IV,* Publication No. 113 (Lafayette, Indiana: Social-Science Education Consortium, 1966), pp. 5–6.

PIAGETIAN PRINCIPLES

1. *Probabilistic reasoning*—the notion that combinations of insufficient causes can render a conclusion more likely to occur—is a cognitive prerequisite for learning.

2. *Multpile classification*—the notion of multiple rationality and hierarchical groupings—is a cognitive prerequisite for learning.

3. *Multiple causation*—the ability to think in terms of natural causes and to conceive of a variety of types of causes; the ability to regard an event or series of events as being generated by a prior event or series of events —is a cognitive prerequisite for learning.

4. *Conservation of invariants*—the idea that certain things stand still or remain constant even though some of their characteristics may be altered —is a cognitive prerequisite for learning.

SOCIAL-SCIENCE LEARNING

The basic uncertainty about the accuracy of historical predictions of conclusions. The conception of outcomes as the product of identifiable determinants plus chance elements.

Data such as government tables of organizations, authority relations, and taxonomic classifications and role-hierarchies.

The causal relationship of historical phenomena; a notion of multiple-causality; and the notion of causes continuously operating across extended time periods.

The possibility of generalizations about historical processes that are applicable to a variety of different events.

Let us take an important social science event—the American Revolution. In connection with this particular event, the first thoughts that come to mind may be associations such as revolution, England, George Washington, thirteen colonies, independence, and Jefferson. The reader may select other attributes of this event, each one of which may denote a class concept; for example, time, geography, and colonization. There may be differences in the attributes selected by the author and the reader, but commonalities will also appear, because the author and the reader share a common educational and cultural experience.

•   •   •   •   •   •   •   •   •   •   •   •   •   •   •   •

What we have done . . . is to identify a set of criterial attributes which define a part of the totality. This labeling of attributes we call *multiple labeling*.

An awareness of the range of attributes or aspects of any instance is a crucial prerequisite for the development of more complex classification behaviors. If we are able to specify many labels, we can classify instances in many categories. Thus, for example, . . . we could categorize the American Revolution under the class "revolution," or "independence," or "anti-British," or "war," and so on.

The number and kind of instances that can be brought under a particular heading depends on the criterial attribute selected. Thus, for the class "fruit," we could include such objects as pears and oranges; but if our criterial attribute were the class "red," we would select additional instances possessing the attribute "red." Similarly, we could construct a class, "wars on the American continent," including the American Revolution, the Civil War and the War of

1812; and we could construct a class, "British-American wars," including the American Revolution and the War of 1812, but excluding the Civil War.

• • • • • • • • • • • • • • • • • •

The ability to combine two or more attributes is a very significant one in the logical development of thought; it is a prototype of complex thinking, in which classes are combined and recombined as the needs of the problem dictate. In the process of combining and recombining a group of items, a child has to shift his criteria; flexibility is required in the manipulation of multiple criteria.

Sigel goes on to note how, in order to deal with problems of multiple classification and interdependence of attributes, a youngster must be capable of performing two mental operations, reversibility and reciprocity.[45]

Reversibility is a mental operation in which materials or ideas are reorganized so as to reconstruct the original state or class.

• • • • • • • • • • • • • • • • • •

A social science illustration of reversibility is the case of dollars which can be changed into British pounds, and then converted back into dollars. The value of the dollar, or the value of the money in question, has been conserved even though it appears in a different form. Also if the money is changed into other denominations, such as smaller coins or smaller bills, the amount is still the same.

Reciprocity connotes an interaction between things. For example, in economics, reciprocal relationships are evident when one country reduces tariffs and the other country involved sells it more goods. As applied to this specific case, the principle is that tariffs are related to the amount of goods bought and sold. An increase in tariffs causes a decrease in trade, while a decrease in tariffs leads to an increase in trade. There is a reciprocal relationship between trade and tariffs . . .

Probably the best known application of some of Piaget's findings to social-studies instruction and curriculum design was made by the late Hilda Taba and her associates. Their conclusions relating to concept learning in the social studies have been reported in two studies, *Thinking in Elementary School Children*[46] and *Teaching Strategies and Cognitive Functioning in Elementary School Children.*[47] One of the more provocative relevant findings of their studies was that "slow learners" were capable of abstract thinking under a program of instruction that regulates assimilation according to student needs and that allows ample opportunities for concrete operations before making a transition to abstract operations and symbolic content.[48]

---

[45] *Ibid.,* pp. 8–9.

[46] Taba *et al., op. cit.*

[47] Hilda Taba, *Teaching Strategies and Cognitive Functioning in Elementary School Children,* Cooperative Research Project No. 2404 (Washington, D.C.: U. S. Office of Education), 1966.

[48] Taba *et al., op. cit.,* p. 176.

Taba *et al.* in *Thinking in Elementary School Children* summarized their conclusions concerning the structuring of learning experiences for concept development in the social studies:[49]

> There should also be a sequence in learning experiences so that each preceding step develops the skills which are prerequisite for the next step. For example, because the transition from concrete to operational thinking is of especial importance for school age children, the sequence of school experiences should begin with experiences with concrete objects, materials to facilitate description, analysis, and differentiation. The early years of school may need to concentrate on providing abundant experience in manipulation and combining, matching, and grouping objects in order to facilitate the mastery of concrete thinking. Opportunities for the active processing of information may provide the necessary conditions for the evolution and organization of abstract conceptual schemes. This preparation lays the groundwork for formal thinking, for manipulation of abstract symbols, and for the capacity to discover relationships between objects and events.

RESEARCH SUMMARIES

A variety of basic generalizations concerning procedures for effecting classroom concept learning, some based on laboratory studies and some based on classroom studies, has been developed by Woodruff.[50] He concludes that:[51]

1. The basic process by which one acquires concepts of specific objects or events is the same for all concepts and for all students.
2. All of the things in a given class can be learned by one general kind of learning experience.
3. A student is prepared to acquire a new concept when he already has a store of concepts appropirate to understanding the new concepts.
4. Lessons contribute most to the progress of students when each one introduces one significant concept abstracted from a sequence of concepts, assuming that other learning factors are satisfactory.
5. The presentation of several concepts in a single lesson is confusing to students and learning proceeds more rapidly when concepts are presented singly.

Finally, Robert Glaser, in a succinct summary of the literature on concept learning and teaching, has concluded:[52]

> We know something about concepts consisting of nonverbal dimensions where the stimulus values are perceptually clear, and where the instance-non-instance boundaries are reasonably clear, and further, where such concepts involve rules that are taught by an inductive procedure. This kind of concept

---

[49] *Ibid.*, p. 22.

[50] Asahel D. Woodruff, *Basic Concepts of Teaching, Concise ed.* (Scranton, Pa.: Chandler, 1961).

[51] Woodruff, *op. cit.*, pp. 7–9, 115.

[52] Glaser, *op. cit.*, p. 27.

task seems to define the situation that prevails in two cases: (1) in non-verbal tasks and in concept learning with pre-verbal learners, that is, young children; this kind of situation is exemplified by the inductive learning of such concepts as triangle, quadrilateral, and circle; and (2) tasks for verbal learners where a concept to be learned is intricate to verbalize so that it needs to be learned by induction from exemplars . . .

NEGLECTED AREAS OF RESEARCH ON CONCEPT LEARNING

In a paper cited earlier,[53] Frayer and Klausmeier suggested that:

Additional research should be carried out to establish the generality of the effect of emphasis of relevant attribute values and to determine other variables which may improve learning from texts. The value of this research strategy is that variables may be identified which could be incorporated into instructional material in many subject-matter areas.

Similarly, Glaser outlined seven key neglected research areas, based upon his recent survey of the relevant literature on concept learning.[54] He urges research dealing with:

1. Concepts that are comprised of verbal, thematic, and meaningful dimensions and that involve a mediated response.
2. Concepts with definitional parameters that are altered with increased experience and knowledge.
3. Concepts in which the "salience or perceptibility of different dimensions differ as a function of societal norms, differing perceptual characteristics of the stimuli involved, or individual learner histories."
4. Concepts that are relational rather than conjunctive.
5. Concepts that more efficiently might be learned "deductively;" that is, by first stating a rule, then examining exemplars and non-exemplars.
6. Concepts that are based on a hierarchy of previously learned concepts.
7. Concepts "Whose acquisition de-emphasizes memory by providing the learner with a strategy which minimizes memory requirements, or by providing him with tools or job aids for memory storage."

CONCLUSION

In one of the pioneer treatises on cognitive processes, Vinacke sketched much of the framework of contemporary research on concept learning. His treatment of concept-related matters is singularly notable for the problems it outlined in concept research, for the pregnant questions it raised, and for the

---

[53] Frayer and Klausmeier, *op. cit.,* pp. 16–17.

[54] Glaser, *op. cit.,* p. 27. For an extensive bibliography on concept learning, see the two works: Herbert J. Klausmeier *et al. Concept Learning: A Bibliography, 1950–1967.* Technical Report No. 82, Research and Development Center for Cognitive Learning (Madison: University of Wisconsin, 1969); and Herbert J. Klausmeier *et al., A Supplement to Technical Report No. 2, Concept Learning: A Bibliography, 1968,* Technical Report No. 107, Research and Development Center for Cognitive Learning (Madison: University of Wisconsin, 1969).

penetrating criticisms it leveled at existing research. In his book, *Psychology of Thinking,* he suggested the difficulty of selecting classification schema for concepts and outlined some key factors to be considered in the conceptualizing process.[55]

> We must distinguish between the process of forming concepts and the characteristics of concepts themselves. There has been insufficient awareness of this distinction, both in theoretical discussions of the subject and in experimental studies. We need to know what happens during the learning process to explain the acquisition of concepts and also how the resulting cognitive structures function in the mental activity of the individual.

Interestingly, a 1968 article by the Kendlers on "Concept Formation," appearing in the recent edition of the *International Encyclopedia of the Social Sciences,* seems to suggest that we have not made as much progress as might be desired in resolving the substantive concerns that Vinacke highlights.[56]

> There is little doubt that the discrimination process is of primary importance in concept formation. The best method of teaching a concept would be to arrange the optimal conditions for discriminating between instances that belong to a concept and those that do not. Although such a principle would be generally accepted, there would be much disagreement about its specific interpretation. Whether optimal conditions for discrimination could be best arranged by reinforcing correct habits and not reinforcing incorrect ones, by encouraging suitable mediational responses, by training the organism to perceive crucial differences, by developing appropriate cognitive systems, or by some favorable combination of all of these factors—all these issues would be open to dispute. Basic to this agreement are two related questions: Do these apparent differences always represent real differences? If so, does their resolution depend upon their being cast in precise mathematical language?

Moreover, the quotation captures aptly how apparent agreement by researchers on basic principles of concept learning may mask underlying sharp disagreements over appropriate corresponding instructional settings. This phenomenon is the challenge that confronts social studies teachers as they look to research for guidance in structuring lessons.

SUGGESTED READINGS

Ausubel, David P. *Educational Psychology: A Cognitive View*. New York: Holt, 1968, Chap. 15.

> A rigorous, stimulating discussion of classroom-related experimental research on concept learning by the author and others, as well as some theoretical remarks concerning the nature of concepts.

[55] Vinacke, *op. cit.,* p. 98.
[56] Howard H. Kendler and Tracy S. Kendler, "Concept Formation," *International Encyclopedia of the Social Sciences,* vol. 3, L. Sills, ed. (New York: Macmillan and Free Press, 1968), p. 210.

Bruner, Jerome S., Jacqueline J. Goodnow, and George Austin. *A Study of Thinking.* New York: Science Editions, 1962.

A major work dealing with a variety of experimental and theoretical issues associated with the nature of cognitive processes.

Gagné, Robert M. *The Conditions of Learning.* New York: Holt, 1965.

A highly readable, complete analysis of the author's views on learning, with a systematic discussion of each of the eight possible conditions for learning that he postulates.

Glaser, Robert. "Concept Learning and Concept Teaching." *Learning Research and School Subjects,* Robert M. Gagné and William J. Gephart, eds. Itasca, Ill.: Peacock, 1969.

Succinct and lucid summary of possible instructional applications of selected concept-learning research and a delineation of major areas in which further research is required.

Hooper, Frank H. "Piagetian Research and Education." *Logical Thinking in Children,* Irving E. Sigel and Frank H. Hooper, eds. New York: Holt, 1968.

Summarizes instruction-related research concerning Piaget's theories, with a special section dealing with the social studies.

Ripple, Richard E., and Verne N. Rockcastle, eds. *Piaget Rediscovered.* Cooperative Research Project No. F-040. Washington, D.C.: U.S. Office of Education, 1964.

Series of excellent papers from a symposium dealing with the work of Piaget and his Geneva associates. Of particular interest are papers by Piaget and Peel.

Sax, Gilbert, "Concept Formation." *Encyclopedia of Educational Research,* 4th edition, Robert L. Ebel, ed. New York: Macmillan, 1969.

Well-organized summary of research relating to concept learning, with a particularly good coverage of the social-studies area.

CHAPTER 4

Research Applied to Teaching Social-Science Concepts, Preschool-12: The Parameters of Concepts

There is a firm belief that no social-studies lesson can proceed without a common conceptual linkage between teacher and students. That thousands of lessons taught daily throughout the United States ignore this basic axiom, does not invalidate its spirit. The key notion at stake concerns conceptual interaction and growth rather than mere verbal interaction, as Vygotsky reminds us:[1]

> True human communication presupposes a generalizing attitude, which is an advanced stage in the development of word meanings. The higher forms of human intercourse are possible only because man's thought reflects conceptualized actuality. That is why certain thoughts cannot be communicated to children even if they are familiar with the necessary words. The adequately generalized concept that alone ensures full understanding may still be lacking. Tolstoy, in his educational writings, says that children often have difficulty in learning a new word not because of its sound but because of the concept to which the word refers.

SYMBOLS VERSUS CONCEPTS

Symbol transmission, of course, can and does proceed in many social-studies classes without common conceptual referents. Students may use terms such as "39th parallel," "black power," "democracy," or "justice," either verbally or in writing, and still be conceptually ignorant of their basic meanings. A student quickly learns that the transmission of symbols will often pass for "learn-

---

[1] L. S. Vygotsky, *Thought and Language,* Eugenia Hoffman and Gertrude Vakar, ed. and trans. (Cambridge, Massachusetts: M. I. T. Press, 1962), p. 7.

ing," in the conceptual sense, in the classroom or in society at large. Both examinations and casual conversation with elders, he finds, frequently place emphasis upon symbol transmission and recognition rather than conceptualizing. Granted, there are hierarchical *levels* of symbol interaction that are expected, and these grow increasingly complex and sophisticated as one proceeds to graduate-level training.

The basic emphasis, however, frequently remains upon the manipulation of symbols as an end in itself rather than as a vehicle or tool to conceptualize. Sigel comments upon the educational implications of this phenomenon:[2]

> The use of language and interpretation of language in the socioeducational context deserves special attention. The teacher must be sensitive to the child's capacity for assimilating verbal language as well as be aware of the relationship between the child's language and his thought. . . . the child's correct contextual use of a term is not necessarily indicative of his comprehension of that term or an accurate reflection of the child's ability to understand the logical basic of the concept.

Thus, symbols often take on a *situational* meaning apart from their conceptual meaning. A shrewd student confronted with a question from his teacher such as, "What do you like best about our country?" may discover that he can ease his conceptual burden by replying, "Our democratic process." By doing so, he reflects his grasp of the situational meaning of the term "democratic process," indicating he recognizes these symbols can be positively related to characteristics of the United States. The fact that the student may attach no conceptual meaning to the term is unimportant here because he will probably be rewarded with "That's a good answer, Johnny!" from the teacher. He may even have learned from sad experience that an honest attempt to grapple conceptually with the question in the form of an answer, "Hot dogs, scary movies, and baseball," is frowned upon by the teacher, who categorizes this latter response as "silly." Situationally silly, perhaps, but conceptually pregnant with meaning. Ausubel speaks about this point:[3]

> One reason why pupils commonly develop a rote learning set in relation to potentially meaningful subject matter is because they learn from sad experience that substantively correct answers lacking in verbatim correspondence to what they have been taught receive no credit whatsoever from certain teachers. Another reason is that because of a generally high level of anxiety, or because of chronic failure experience in a given subject (reflective, in turn, of low aptitude or poor teaching), they lack confidence in their ability to learn meaningfully, and hence perceive no alternative to panic apart from rote learning. (This phenomenon is very familiar to mathematics teachers because of

[2] Irving E. Sigel, "The Piagetian System and the World of Education," *Studies in Cognitive Development: Essays in Honor of Jean Piaget,* David Elkind and John H. Flavell, eds. (New York: Oxford University Press, 1969), p. 475.

[3] David P. Ausubel, *Educational Psychology: A Cognitive View* (New York: Holt, 1968), pp. 37–38.

the widespread prevalence of "number shock" or "number anxiety.") Lastly, pupils may develop a rote learning set if they are under excessive pressure to exhibit glibness, or to conceal, rather than admit and gradually remedy, original lack of genuine understanding. Under these circumstances it seems easier and more important ot create a spurious impression of facile comprehension by rotely memorizing a few key terms or sentences, than to try to understand what they mean. Teachers frequently forget that pupils become very adept at using abstract terms with apparent appropriateness—when they have to— even though their understanding of the underlying concepts is virtually non-existent.

Ausubel's point is well-illustrated by young children who are able to distinguish their right hand from their left, but who have no notion of "right" or "left." Very small youngsters learn the symbol game quickly, as they discover that certain terms, spoken in certain contexts, evoke approval or disapproval from parents in the form of smiles, laughter, frowns, or other reinforcements. From the world around them, youngsters are aware at a very early age that symbols have meaning apart from their conceptual relationship; not surprisingly, when this phenomenon later confronts them in classroom situations, it appears quite natural. For, as John Dewey long ago observed, "adults and children alike are capable of using even precise verbal formulae with only the vaguest and most confused sense of what they mean."

A recent cartoon showed an Eskimo parent and child sitting in an igloo reading the nursery rhyme about "Little Jack Horner"; the caption was "What's a corner, Daddy?" The humor of the cartoon derives, in part at least, from the fact that nursery rhymes, much like beer jingles, are frequently regarded as having *situational* rather than *conceptual* import. One need not know what curds and whey are to enjoy Miss Muffett's tale, so the argument goes.

The Eskimo youngster illustrates clearly what occurs when *conceptual* versus *situational* meaning is at issue. Conceptually, he requires an experiential basis, which he now lacks, in order to assimilate his new datum. In effect, he refused to treat the symbolic content as "just part of a nursery rhyme."

Vygotsky has perceived the foregoing issue in the framework of "scientific" versus "pseudo" concepts.[4] "Scientific concepts," which Vygotsky regards as cognitive groupings arranged according to a system of subordinate or of superordinate groupings, correspond to the notion of "conceptual meaning." "Pseudo concepts," which are not developed spontaneously by the child and which are frequently learned by imitation or definition, correspond to "situational meaning." "Pseudo concepts" often mislead teachers and researchers," Taba has observed, "because the superficial similarity of the pseudo concept and of the real concept makes it difficult to distinguish them."[5]

[4] Vygotsky, *op. cit.*, pp. 75–77.
[5] Hilda Taba, *Teaching Strategies and Cognitive Functioning in Elementary School Children,* Cooperative Research Project No. 2404 (Washington, D.C.: U. S. Office of Education, 1966), p. 5.

The relationship to social-studies classrooms and the import of conceptual versus linguistic manipulation for learning may now be clear. In the "nursery rhyme" sense, instruction *can* proceed with little concern for common conceptual referents; "democracy," "justice," *et al.* merely become the equivalents of "curds and whey." To the extent that teachers are sensitive to the need to have a common experiential basis with students in order to proceed with instruction, they, like the Eskimo parent, must answer before they move. "Practical experience also shows," Vygotsky reminds us, "that direct teaching of concepts is impossible and fruitless. A teacher who tries to do this usually accomplishes nothing but empty verbalism, a parrotlike repetition of words by the child, simulating a knowledge of the corresponding concepts but actually covering up a vacuum."[6]

PARAMETERS OF CONCEPTS

Ausubel tells us, "Anyone who pauses long enough to give the problem some serious thought cannot escape the conclusion that man lives in a world of concepts rather than a world of objects, events, and situations. . . . Reality, figuratively speaking, is experienced through a conceptual or categorical filter."[7] His message serves as a sharp reminder of the enormous compression of data that occurs when we communicate with concepts. His example of sighting a "house" is a good case in point.[8]

> When someone, for example, tells us that he sees a "house," he is not really communicating his *actual* experience, but a highly simplified and generalized version of it—an interpretation that reflects the cultural consensus regarding the essential (criterial, identifying) attributes of "house." His *actual* conscious experience of the event is infinitely more particularistic with respect to size, shape, style, hue, brightness, and presumed cost than the message communicated by his generic use of the term "house." If he actually tried to communicate his detailed cognitive experience, it would not only take him half a day, but he would still also be unable completely to express in words many of its more subtle nuances.

Rules, Attributes, and Exemplars

Concepts may be thought of as a category of experience having (a) a *rule* which defines the relevant category, (b) a set of *positive instances* or *exemplars* with *attributes,* and (c) a *name* (though this latter element is sometimes missing). Thus, "a natural elevation of the earth's surface rising to a summit" is a rule stating essential or criterial attributes with the name "mountain," of which "Fuji" is a positive illustration or exemplar. Rules then, are the formulae or statements in symbolic form specifying the criterial attributes of the category.

[6] Vygotsky, *op. cit.,* p. 8.
[7] Ausubel, *op. cit.,* p. 505.
[8] *Ibid.,* pp. 505–506.

Attributes, in turn, are those characteristics which are the identifying features of a concept and which enable one to distinguish between exemplars and non-exemplars. Exemplars may be regarded as instances of the concept; nonexemplars as negative examples; and names as symbols commonly used by a culture to identify or label a concept.

The importance of phrasing rules in a language appropriate for the student's age level should be underscored, since many of the problems connected with concept learning derive from linguistic barriers. Henry Johnson provides us with an apt anecdote on this point:[9]

> Was the seventh grade girl who came home from a history lesson reporting that "General Arnold cut off both of General Burgoyne's legs" exercising her fool spot or was the fool spot in the textbook which informed her that "General Arnold cut off General Burgoyne's supporting column?"

Translatability of rules into the youngster's linguistic dimensions becomes a significant constraint in selecting social-science concepts for teaching. Language, of course, has long been considered to have a key causal relationship with concept learning. As Sapir eloquently phrased it, "Language is a dynamo that we use principally for lighting little name plates, for labelling and categorizing things." Worf's pioneer linguistic analyses similarly underscored how man is language-bound in all his intellectual activities. But, while vocabulary and concept development have a close relationship, it is one of contingency rather than equivalency, as has been indicated.

Neither naming a concept nor stating its corresponding rule guarantees, however, that one can identify exemplars of the concept. This qualification distinguishes symbol transmission from conceptualizing. An individual demonstrates minimal attainment of a concept when he can identify instances of a concept and distinguish them from noninstances with high reliability. Robert Gagné made a similar point in his book, *The Conditions of Learning*:[10]

> Regardless of what stimuli have been used for learning, the acquisition of the concept *odd* is tested by presenting a stimulus situation that has not been involved in the learning. Similarly for *edge*, or *raise* or any other concept. There must be a demonstration that the learner can generalize the concept to a variety of specific instances of the class that have not been used in learning. Otherwise, it is not a concept, but merely a collection of specific chains.

The rule is what Hunt and Metcalf refer to as the *intension* of a concept as opposed to its *extension*, which is the set of items to which it is applied.[11] They

---

[9] Henry Johnson, *The Teaching of History*, rev. ed. (New York: Macmillan, 1940), p. 249.

[10] Robert M. Gagné, *The Conditions of Learning* (New York: Holt, 1965), p. 136.

[11] Maurice P. Hunt and Lawrence E. Metcalf, *Teaching High School Studies: Problems in Reflective Thinking and Social Understanding*, 2d ed. (New York: Harper, 1968), p. 89. Also see David Elkind, "Conservation and Concept Formation," *Studies in Cognitive Development: Essays in Honor of Jean Piaget*, David Elkind and John H. Flavell, eds. (New York: Oxford University Press, 1969), pp. 180–181.

cite the Beardsley example of "city:" "The extension of 'city' is London, Paris, New York, Berlin, Tokyo, Moscow, Nairobi, etc. The intension of 'city' is (roughly) the characteristic of being a politically independent area of high population density and large population total."[12]

Hunt and Metcalf also call attention to the characteristic of personal and official definitions of concepts. They suggest that, in general, teachers eschew personally held definitions whenever possible and opt instead for the definitions conventionally attached by social-science scholars. The qualification they add, however, is important to note:[13]

> The superiority of official definitions over most personal definitions does not mean that a teacher should have no interest in students' personal definitions. Asking for personal definitions is a practice that helps a teacher acquaint himself with the backgrounds of students. A teacher might ask each of his students to write a paper on "What Democracy Means to Me."

A Concept of a Concept

Much of the controversy surrounding appropriate procedures for teaching social-science concepts stems from the rendering of concepts within the social-science disciplines into verbal representations in the classroom. "Certainly two of the most critical decisions involved in attempting to teach a subject matter," Gardner and Johnson state:[14]

> Are the manner in which its domain of concepts (i.e., its content) is to be sampled and how the concepts within a given sample are to be arranged for instructional purposes . . . The structure of a behavioral science does not itself indicate how decisions concerning the sampling and arrangement of its concepts are to be made, and the nature of the relationship between the logical structure of the subject matter of a discipline and its representation in instruction is ultimately a psychology rather than a logical matter.

While "structure" may suggest logical modes for organizing data for learning, conceptualizing is a psychological phenomenon with its own unique logical dynamics. What is required by the teacher, in effect, is a concept of a concept which permits him to make inferences about appropriate pedagogical procedures. In this spirit, a definition is suggested which draws heavily upon the work of Bruner *et al.*[15] and Viaud:[16]

---

[12] *Ibid.,* p. 89, as quoted from Monroe C. and Elizabeth L. Beardsley, *Philosophical Thinking: An Introduction* (New York: Harcourt, 1965), p. 24.

[13] *Ibid.,* p. 90.

[14] William E. Gardner and Paul E. Johnson, "Language Habits in the Behavioral Sciences, Their Role and Representation in Instruction," unpublished paper, University of Minnesota, 1968.

[15] Jerome S. Bruner, Jacqueline J. Goodnow, and George Austin, *A Study of Thinking* (New York: Science Editions, 1962), p. 244.

[16] Gaston Viaud, *Intelligence: Its Evolution and Form,* E. J. Pomerans, trans. (New York: Harper, 1960); see pp. 75–76 for the development of his definition.

A concept is a continuum of inferences by which a set of observed characteristics of an object or event suggests a class identity, and then additional inferences about other unobserved characteristics of the object or event.

By "suggests" it is meant that the organism involved is prompted to go beyond the immediate objects or events perceived, in the sense that inferences are made from what is directly observed. In turn, these inferences suggest additional ones to the organism. To illustrate: One reads in a text, for example, that country A has been externally controlled by country B; from this statement the reader correctly or incorrectly infers "imperialism," which in turn suggests economic, political, and social domination of country A by B, and specifically, the loss of country A's sovereignty. Similarly, if smoke is observed and crackling heard, one may quickly infer "fire," which suggests in turn something-to-be-avoided, the decomposition of matter, and flames—the latter further suggesting water and the need to escape and to seek assistance.

In these two cases, the report of the external control of the country and the sensing of smoke and crackling provided a set of observed characteristics, which suggested a class identity, denoted by a symbol, and then a chain of inferences from observed and unobserved properties.

An essential implication of the definition is that one can only accurately speak of concept Y that person X may have, or of the symbol—let it be called $f(y)$—which stands in place of or suggests Y for X or other persons. To illustrate: if $f(Y) = $ democracy, then for X, $f(Y)$ may stand in place of a series of inter-related ideas dealing with voting, values, power, and the like which make up Y. Those who are unable to infer Y from $f(Y)$ or a similar cue may be said to be potential acquirers of Y, but at that point, the concept is *nonexistent* for them.

A further implication is that concepts do not lie fallow in some mental cavity of an organism, nor are they, strictly speaking, "carried around," strung together," or "held" by organisms. Rather, concepts assume an emergent character and come into being for the organism as immediate perceptions lead to a classification process and eventually to a network of inferences, based on past and present experiences. Prior to the initiation of the network of inferences, the concept in question is momentarily nonexistent for the organism.

Abraham Kaplan distinguishes between concepts and *conceptions*—the later referring to one's particular application or interpretation of a concept.[17]

> A conception "belongs to" a particular person (though, of course, others may have very similar conceptions), and it will differ, in general, from time to time. My conceptions of an atom is different from a nuclear physicist's, largely because of ignorance, and different again from what it was before I was aware of nuclear reactions. Associated with the *usage* of a term is a *concept*, which may be said correspondingly to be a family of conceptions.

Granting the personal nature of an individual's concepts, the concepts that students have which are identified by a common symbol should be essentially

[17] Abraham Kaplan, *The Conduct of Inquiry* (Scranton, Pa.: Chandler, 1964), pp. 48–49.

similar insofar as their critical attributes are shared in common. As Carroll has observed, it is probably a fact that people universally share certain properties in their concepts of such things as sun and man, for example, even though terminology and extended, descriptive features and interrelationships will vary.[18] It seems that it is *critical attributes* of concepts that people share in common when they are able to meaningfully discuss their daily affairs. A professor, for example, probably has a different concept of *automobile* than the garageman who repairs it, but some agreement on the critical attributes of their concepts normally exists, enough so that the professor realizes that he can avail himself of the repairman's services under certain conditions and that both can successfully communicate about the problem. At a different level, since the automobile has become such an engrained element in the American ethos, it is likely that all Americans, drivers and nondrivers, share at an early age at least some critical or essential attributes in their concepts of *automobile,* such as "it is a motorized object that can move one from place to place."

It would appear that the *initial* goal for the teacher is to enable all the students in a class to acquire the critical attributes of a particular concept. Beyond this point, of course, provisions may be made for individual enlargement of the concept. The past experiences of the individual student, the way in which these experiences relate to new ones in the classroom, and the general reaction of students to the teaching situation, among other things, will influence the specific kind of concept that each student acquires.

CONCEPTS AND GENERALIZATIONS

The stuff from which ideas are spun in the social sciences is a mixed bag of intellectual phenomena. No small part of the confusion within the field of social-studies curriculum has resulted from the failure to distinguish clearly between concepts and generalizations as instructional goals and the corresponding instructional procedures necessary to generate them. Until such distinctions have been made, there can be little progress toward developing curricular materials and learning contexts optimally appropriate for the specific cognitive task delineated.

Edith West has suggested the following relationship between concepts, generalizations, and theories:[19]

> Generalizations and theories are built up of specified realtionships among concepts. Moreover, a new term or concept is developed to represent a newly discovered relationship among older concepts. For example, someone notes that

---

[18] John B. Carroll, "Words, Meanings, and Concepts," *Harvard Educational Review,* XXXIV (Spring, 1964), 184.

[19] Edith West, "Concepts, Generalizations, and Theories: Background Paper #3," unpublished paper, Project Social Studies, University of Minnesota, no date, p. 4.

a number of different categories have certain characteristics in common. He invents a new name to represent categories with these attributes (*e.g.,* Groups such as families and friendship groups are characterized by intimate face-to-face relations. The term "primary group" was invented to refer to all groups with this characteristic.) Or a scientist discovers a causal explanation. . . . In this sense, the concept becomes a short-hand notation for an explanatory law.

Her analysis of the relationship is essentially the same as that of Brownell and Hendrickson. The latter contend that any generalization states some abstract relationship among several concepts and that, as such, it is more complex than any single component concept.[20] They argue that teachers should not attempt to teach generalizations among concepts that are not in themselves "meaningful," i.e., concepts that are clearly formulated, understood, and acquired. As a negative example, they offer the generalization, "In a democracy, every citizen is entitled to freedom of worship." If, they state, a child cannot answer such questions as "What is 'freedom of worship?'" and "What is a 'citizen?'" he cannot really acquire the generalization intended.[21]

Vygotsky also called attention to the systematic hierarchical network between concepts that is reflected in generalizations.[22] He provides the illustration of a child who has learned about "flower" and about "rose," but not the supraordinate-subordinate relationship between the two concepts. As the child becomes aware of the nexus between "flower" and "rose," he generates a concept system. "Concepts do not lie in the child's mind like peas in a bag, without any bonds between them" Vygotsky observed.[23]

For purposes of distinguishing, in instructional procedures, the relationship of concept to its complementary intellectual components, let us consider the following schema. *Data* comprise the fabric from which cognitive phenomena evolve. They are normative, they transcend academic disciplinary boundaries, and they constitute the universe of discourse from which knowledge concerning a given topic may be drawn; data represent the unorganized sum total of information. *Facts*, in turn, are a component of data and represent the percentual flow that a given organism generates from data. In this schema they are organized, selective elements of data, as shown in Figure 1.

Fact clusters in a special interrelationship, then, may form a *concept,* as shown in Figure 2 with the category "dog." Figure 2 implies both a structural relationship among F_1, F_2, F_3, and the possibility that F_n may exist. The selection of *three* critical attributes in this illustration is, of course, purely arbitrary. C_1, or any other concept, may have n number of attributes.

Similarly, a hierarchical fact cluster or concept—*animal,* for example—may

---

[20] W. A. Brownell and G. Hendrickson, "How Children Learn Information, Concepts, and Generalizations," *Learning and Instruction, Pt. I, Forty-Ninth Yearbook, National Society for the Study of Education* (Chicago: University of Chicago Press, 1950), pp. 121–122.

[21] *Ibid.*

[22] Vygotsky, *op. cit.,* p. 111.

[23] *Ibid.,* p. 110.

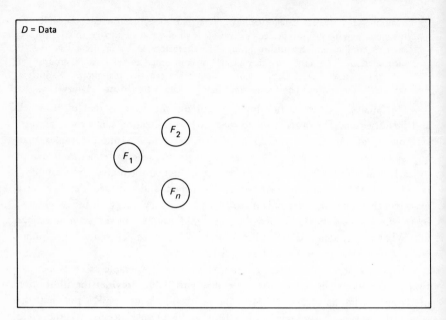

Figure 1. Data and Facts. The relationship of data to facts, where D = all the data pertaining to a particular topic and F_1, F_2, . . . (F_n) = specific facts pertaining to the topic.

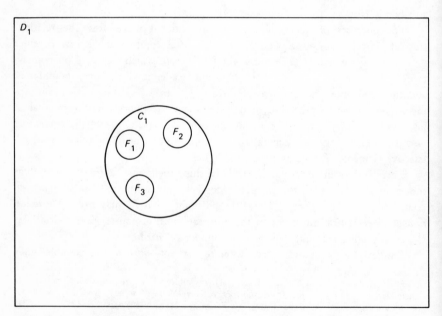

Figure 2. Concept of Dog. The relationship of facts to a concept of "dog" within the context of relevant data, where D_1 = all data relating to dogs C_1 = a concept of dog, and F_1, F_2, F_3 = facts about dogs that represent C_1's criterial attributes.

be considered, as shown in Figure 3. Therein a stated relationship among the concepts *cat, dog,* and animal—for example, "cats and dogs are animals"—forms a very basic *generalization.*[24] At some point in its history, a generalization, once tested and regarded as true, may serve the status of a *fact.* "Cats and dogs are animals," for example, may function as a component of the fact cluster for the concept *pet.*

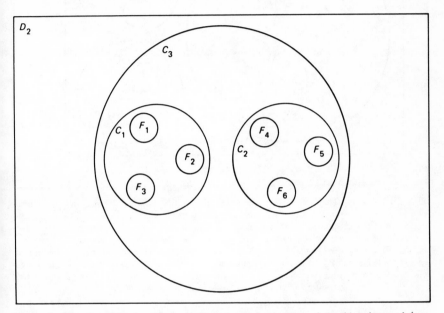

Figure 3. The Generalization: Cats and Dogs Are Animals. The relationship of sets of facts to concepts within the context of relevant data, resulting in a generalization, where $D_2 =$ all data relating to animals, $C_1 =$ a concept of *dog* and F_1, F_2, $F_3 =$ facts about dogs that represent C_1's criterial attributes; $C_2 =$ a concept of *cat* and F_4, F_5, $F_6 =$ facts that represent C_2's criterial attributes; and $C_3 =$ a concept of *animal.*

Finally, a *theory* may be regarded as the set under which related concepts and interrelated fact clusters are subsumed in a special structure. This relationship is illustrated in Figure 4, dealing with the theory "the origin of species."

A similar schema might be devised, for example, for a theory concerning the "origin of cities," where some of the following sample items might be subsumed:

1. *Generalizations:* "All nations have cities." "Cities function as economic units."
2. *Concepts:* city, nation, economy, defense, specialization
3. *Facts:* New York is densely populated; Los Angeles, Philadelphia, and Chicago

---

[24] Gagné refers to this process as "principle learning," instead of the more common term generalization, *op. cit.,* pp. 141–156.

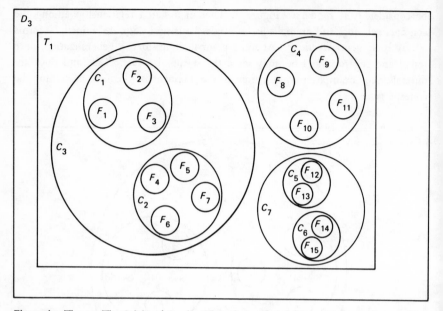

Figure 4. Theory: The Origin of Species. The relationship of facts, concepts, and generalizations to a theory, a subset within the context of relevant data, where D_3 = a set of all data relating to tre origin of species, T_1 = a subset representing a theory on the origin of species, C_1 = a concept of *apes* and F_1, F_2, F_3 = a corresponding fact cluster; C_2 = a concept of *man* and F_4, F_5, F_6, F_7 = a corresponding fact cluster; C_3 = a concept of *animals;* C_4 = a concept of *species* and F_8, F_9, F_{10}, F_{11} = a corresponding fact cluster; C_5 = a concept of *genes* and F_{12}, F_{13} a corresponding fact cluster; C_6 = a concept of *sexual drives* and F_{14}, F_{15} = a corresponding fact cluster; and C_7 = a concept of *reproduction.*

have populations of over two million people. Tokyo is a geographic subdivision of Japan.

4. *Data:* All known phenomena relating to the development of cities.

While these diagrams represent a severe distortion of the actual dynamic relationships in a data-fact-concept-generalization-theory continuum, several points to be considered in organizing concept-learning experiences follow from Figures 1–4.

Each component on the continuum has some subordinate or hierarchical relationship to other components. Concepts are generated from *fact* clusters and, in turn, may organize into *generalizations;* all three comprise the stuff of *theories.* Formation of generalizations presupposes that subsumed concepts already have been learned, and theory acquisition requires the added dimension that a variety of concepts and generalizations be systematically interrelated. This nexus does *not* suggest, however, that the learning of facts must be a discrete step in advance of concept formation. A student may easily be exposed to a plethora of facts concerning government yet never develop a concept. Conversely, however, he must acquire some fact relationship concerning critical attributes of government, if he is to develop a concept.

The popular trend toward rejecting fact-teaching in the social studies, while correct in its general spirit, might be directed more accurately to deemphasizing the accumulation of facts without relationship to their organizing function. What is implicit in much of the worst of social-studies teaching today is a sort of "meat hook" theory of learning, reflecting the notion that facts are "meat" to be stored on "hooks" in the "freezer" of the mind and retrieved someday when required for consumption. As Whitehead observed:[25]

> A single fact in isolation is the primary myth required for finite thought, that is to say, for thought unable to embrace totality.
> This mythological character arises because there is not such fact. Connectedness is of the essence of all things of all types. It is of the essence of all types that they be connected. Abstraction from connectedness involves the omission of an essential factor in the fact considered. No fact is merely itself.

In addition to organizing facts, learning a given concept may concurrently involve learning in advance a subordinate concept. At least one study has indicated that subordinate social science concepts may be learned efficiently in tandem with supraordinate concepts.[26] Whatever the chronology of the learning sequence between concepts, however, clearly it must be a hierarchical one. In a geography-oriented lesson in an elementary class, for example, a teacher may be interested in introducing youngsters to map and globes as models, which can predict phenomena in a real world. She isolates "equator" as the initial concept for students to learn and sets as the concept rule: "an imaginary line around the earth which is everywhere equally distant from the two poles." Unfortunately for the teacher, "poles" and "earth" are two subordinate concepts that many of her students may not have learned, particularly, if this is their first exposure to maps and globes. If she is cognizant of the problem, the teacher may back up and first develop the subordinate concepts. Otherwise, what many students are likely to learn is some variations of the themes: "It's the red line around the globe. It's the place where the halves of the globe are put together. It's the place where it's zero on the map. That's where it's real hot." All these observations might also be facts noted by one who *has learned* the concept, but in isolation they do *not* comprise the criterial attributes stated in the rule.

A variety of data elements may provide the facts from which concepts are constructed. Since the *same* facts need not be interrelated to generate a commonly shared concept, some attention, at least, to the individual differences of students is possible. A teacher, for example, who wishes to develop a concept

[25] A. N. Whitehead, *Modes of Thought* (New York: Macmillan, 1938), pp. 12–13.
[26] John M. Newton and Albert E. Hickey, "Sequence Effects in Programmed Learning of a Verbal Concept," *Journal of Educational Psychology*, LVI (1965), 140–147.

of power need not require students to be restricted to a specific body of social-science facts. Given a concept rule as a guide, the general data-base might be (a) a mayor's office operations in Chicago, (b) Saul Alinsky's programs, (c) Theodore Roosevelt's foreign policies, (d) influence of advertisers on television programming, or (e) Stalin's regime. Self-generating historical parallels are provided at the level of concepts, without the artificial and vague linkage between events that social-studies teachers often laboriously attempt to contrive.

A student's conceptual development is a coefficient of his data-base dimensions. While the selective organization of facts provides the main focus for a concept-learning task, it is important not to overlook the obvious role of the leaner's data base. Typically, it may have several dimensions: (a) teacher's background; (b) student's background; (c) classroom materials; (d) nonclassroom materials or data from home, mass media, etc. All the dimensions have limitations for a concept-learning task in that they already represent a *filtering* of data or a store of *facts*. Consequently, the teacher reflects rather her *fact-base*, as does the student, as do curricular materials by reflecting the author's *fact-base*, and as do the news media. The greater the screening out of relevant data, as represented, for example, by experience-deprived teachers, students, curricular materials, and nonclassroom materials, the more restricted is the student's opportunity to develop a given concept. This is the point that the historian Carl L. Becker makes:

> If our memories of past events are short and barren, our anticipations of future events will be short and barren; if our memories are rich and diversified, our anticipations of what is to come are likely to be more or less so, too. But the main point is that the character of the pattern of the one, no less than its richness and extent, will depend on the character of the other.[27]

Much of the criticism of the treatment of concepts related to "black history" may be viewed in this perspective. The argument that the curriculum and the instruction have ignored and/or systematically distorted the black experience, and consequently spawned ill-formed concepts about some minorities and neglected others, may be seen as a criticism of the narrow data base provided for students. In a recent *Harper's* article, Bayard Rustin put the argument neatly: "The history of the black man in America has been scandalously distorted in the past, and as a field of study it has been relegated to a second-class status, isolated from the main themes of American history and omitted in the historical education of American youth."[28]

The notion of data as discrete from facts suggests that students and teachers should be more sensitive to broadening their data-seeking tools and to rejecting facile fact compilation as an end. In the process of facilitating concept learning, a

---

[27] Carl L. Becker, *The Heavenly City of the Eighteenth-Century Philosophers* (New Haven, Conn.: Yale University Press, 1932), p. 121.
[28] Bayard Rustin, "The Failure of Black Separatism," *Harper's,* CCXL (January, 1970), 30.

teacher will assist students in acquiring the skills necessary for extending the dimensions of their data base as widely as possible. This approach, for example, would enable students to see their's and others' daily life experience flow as a pregnant source of social-science data. In this sense, they might perceive themselves in their cultural interactions as data generators, as well as receivers, and become more sensitive to the data limitations of all curricular materials.

DIMENSIONS OF CONCEPT LEARNING

The process of concept learning may be viewed as involving primarily the abstracting of the essential fundamental features of a class of items or events that otherwise vary in noncriterial attributes and the translating of them into a cognitive structure. Hunt and Metcalf suggest, for example, that "it is convenient to think for four levels of concept learning: recognition, classification, definition, and generalization."[29]

The psychological processes involved in the highest form of concept formation, Ausubel has advanced in a thorough analysis, include the following exhaustive list of components:[30] (1) discriminating different stimulus patterns: (2) formulating hypotheses relating to abstracted common elements; (3) subsequent testing of such hypotheses in specific situations; (4) designating some of these into a general category or set of common attributes that covers all possible variations; (5) relating these attributes to similar ideas; (6) discriminating the new concept from similar concepts learned earlier; (7) generalizing the criterial attributes of the new concept to all members of the class; and (8) representing the new categorical content with a symbol commonly used in our culture.

Generalization of the criterial or critical attributes to all members of the class requires the learner to generalize among exemplars presented in a particular learning task, as well as to other exemplars he will encounter in the future. Stereotypes, for example, present an extreme example of *overgeneralization,* in which the learner has formed rigid concepts that do not assimilate and accommodate experience. A teacher's role in these situations is to initiate the process of qualifying such overgeneralizations by presenting new and objective information for concept modification. As DeCecco suggests:[31]

> If the child excludes members of some races, religions, and nationalities from the general concept *human being,* some instruction is strongly indicated. Or, if the child lists the attributes of one race as intelligent, socially responsible, sanitary, and achieving and the attributes of another race as stupid, irrespon-

---

[29] Hunt and Metcalf, *op. cit.,* p. 91.
[30] Ausubel, *op. cit.,* p. 517.
[31] John P. DeCecco, *The Psychology of Learning and Instruction* (Englewood Cliffs, N. J.: Prentice-Hall, 1968), p. 400.

sible, dirty, and lazy, the teacher can provide a wider array of positive and negative examples for both races than the child may have experienced before.

Vygotsky, whose work represented a pioneer effort, examined the dimensions of concept learning from a developmental point of view.[32]

> The principal findings of our study may be summarized as follows: The development of the processes which eventually result in concept formation begins in earliest childhood, but the intellectual functions that in a specific combination form the psychological basis of the process of concept formation ripen, take shape, and develop only at puberty. Before that age, we find certain intellectual formations that perform functions similar to those of the genuine concepts to come . . .
>
> Concept formation is the result of a complex activity in which all the basic intellectual functions take part. The process cannot, however, be reduced to association, attention, imagery, inference, or determining tendencies. They are all indispensable, but they are insufficient without the use of the sign, or word, as the means by which we direct our mental operations, control their course, and channel them toward the solution of the problem confronting us.
>
> • • • • • • • • • • • • • • • • • •
>
> The young child takes the first step toward concept formation when he puts together a number of objects in an *unorganized congeries,* or "heap," in order to solve a problem that we adults would normally solve by forming a new concept. The heap, consisting of disparate objects grouped together without any of the sign (artificial word) to inherently unrelated objects linked by chance in the child's perception.

CONCLUSION

The major import for the classroom teacher of a multidimensional perspective of concept learning is that instructional strategies require a sequential pattern that takes into account not only a logical analysis of the subject matter relationship but also the cognitive, affective, and developmental state of the learner.

SUGGESTED READINGS

Ausubel, David P. *Educational Psychology: A Cognitive View.* New York: Holt, 1968, Chap. 15.

Fine analysis of the dimensions of concept learning from both an experimental and a general theoretical viewpoint.

Bruner, Jerome S., Jacqueline J. Goodnow, and George A. Austin, *A Study of Thinking.* New York: Science Editions, 1962.

[32] Vygotsky, *op. cit.,* pp. 58–68.

A major work dealing with a variety of experimental and theoretical issues associated with the nature of cognitive processes. Considerable attention is paid to the role of symbolling in concept learning.

Vygotsky, L. S. *Thought and Language*. Eugenia Hanfmann and Gertrude Vakar, eds. and transl. Cambridge, Mass.: M.I.T. Press, 1962.

A pionner study dealing with the role of language in the formation of concepts. The clear analysis is particularly relevant for teachers.

West, Edith. "Concepts, Generalizations, and Theories: Background Paper #3." Unpublished paper, Project Social Studies, University of Minnesota, no date.

Perhaps the only theoretical discussion by a major social-studies project of the distinctions between concepts and other cognitive processes and the implications for classroom instruction.

CHAPTER 5

Research Applied to Teaching Social-Science Concepts, Preschool-12: Instructional Strategies and the Curriculum

INDUCTIVE VERSUS DEDUCTIVE APPROACHES

Much of the recent discussion about instructional strategies has been filtered through the perspective of *inductive* or discovery and *deductive* approaches. The term *inductive* generally means that the learner is allowed (or forced) to infer conclusions from a basic fact base presented to him. In some forms of this approach the conclusions are predetermined, and the fact basis provided is strung-out sequentially in steps for a learner. Hilda Taba reflects this analysis in her statement:[1]

> Inductive learning requires inductive teaching. Inductive teaching, in turn requires the projection of a sequence of learning experiences by thinking backward: by determining what the students need to start with in order to end up with the expected concept, generalization, or intellectual skill. This projection of sequential learning experiences must also be cumulative in its impact, in the sense of starting with what students already know, understand, or can conceptualize and proceeding in an ascending hierarchy to the more complex and abstract ideas and the more demanding mental operations and inquiry techniques.

A deductive approach, on the other hand, parallels the process of deductive reasoning. Commonly, it involves presenting a conclusion or rule and then attempting to verify it through the repeated illustration of appropriate facts. In a concept-learning task, according to the former approach, a learner would be required minimally to infer a rule for categorizing facts into a conceptual

[1] Hilda Taba, "Techniques of In-Service Training," *Social Education,* XXIX (November, 1965), 472.

network from a series of positive and/or negative instances of a concept. The latter approach requires minimally an initial statement of the concept attributes, accompanied by appropriate exemplars and/or nonexemplars of the concept.

While considerable research energy has been expended on the general question of the relative merits of inductive versus deductive teaching procedures, no categorical claims for the superiority of either approach can be made for the area of social studies. As Wittrock notes in a recent review of the literature, it "precludes any important considerations about teaching or learning."[2]

This dilemma accrues in part from the fact that few related studies exist that explicitly deal with the social studies. In part, too, it may be seen as the result of experimenters' failures to delineate operationally the nature of their inductive and deductive treatments. This failure, more than any other, is responsible for the lack of *cumulative* knowledge about the two approaches.

Research on Inductive or Discovery Strategies

The serious problems that preclude broad generalizations also concern isolating and analyzing the varied dimensions of learning that may be affected by inductive or deductive approaches. One of the more carefully defined, multifaceted studies comparing the two approaches may illustrate some of these dimensions. Worthen, reporting on a study[3] comparing the effects of both discovery and expository presentations on the learning of mathematical concepts, defines his expository treatment in terms of five sequential steps: interjection of teacher knowledge; introduction of generalization; method of answering questions; control of pupil interaction; and methods of eliminating false concepts. Each step, in turn, has a series of specifications. Similarly, the discovery treatment also has five steps: interjection of teacher knowledge; introduction of generalization; method of answering questions; control of pupil interaction; and method of eliminating false concepts.

To insure that teachers complied with and adhered to the two treatment models, thereby assuring discrete treatments, two measures, an observer rating scale and a pupil questionnaire, were used. Eight criterion measures were then made to determine the different dimensions of learning:

1. a concept-achievement test of initial learning
2. a concept-retention test (at two later points in time)
3. a concept-transfer test (to new situations)
4. a negative concept-transfer test
5. a written, heuristic transfer (abstraction of a principle)

[2] M. C. Wittrock, "The Learning-By-Discovery Hypothesis," *Learning by Discovery: A Critical Appraisal*, Lee S. Shulman and Evan R. Keislar, eds. (Chicago: Rand McNally, 1966), p. 45.

[3] Blaine R. Worthen, "A Study of Discovery and Expository Presentations: Implications for Teaching," *Journal of Teacher Education*, XIX (Summer, 1968), 223–242.

6. an oral, heuristic principle
7. a statement attitude scale (pupil reaction to the subject)
8. a semantic, differential attitude scale.

Worthen's results indicated a variance in the superiority of the two approaches, *according to the dimension of learning isolated*. Apart from the instructional implications of his study, the important lesson for our concern here is that overgeneralization about discovery or inductive versus deductive teaching is likely unless the microvariable manipulated is carefully specified and the results are interpreted in this limited sense. Had Worthen, for example, examined only *initial learning* and generalized to expository and discovery approach, the results would have shown a significant learning difference for the *expository* approach; had he considered only *retention learning,* the *discovery* approach would have been shown to be superior.

By specifying an operational distinction between the two approaches, Worthen also avoids the logic controversy concerning whether induction and deduction may be regarded as discrete processes. Certainly, in social studies the products of inductive reasoning require verification through deduction at some point. Moreover, it is difficult to understand how induction can proceed without a data base grounded on deduction.

Organization of Curricular Materials

The work of Festinger in experiments dealing with cognitive dissonance seems to suggest one clue for teaching strategies appropriate to revising concepts students hold; it also provides a promising paradigm for further experimentation in subject areas.[4] On the basis of his research, Festinger has concluded that if an organism is placed in a situation where two cognitions are psychologically perceived as being in a dissonant relationship with one another, there is a tendency to attempt to modify one's cognitive structure to produce compatibility and thus reduce the dissonance. A general implication from his work, for example, is that teaching strategies which force students to grasp the dissonance between concepts established upon erroneous data may serve to effect concept revision.

This notion is echoed in Sigel's summary of the implications for education of Piaget's research:[5]

[4] Leon Festinger, "The Motivating Effect of Cognitive Dissonance," *The Cognitive Processes,* Robert J. C. Harper *et al.,* eds. (Englewood Cliffs, N.J.: Prentice-Hall, 1964), p. 513. See also his work, *A Theory of Cognitive Dissonance* (New York: Harper, 1957), for a more comprehensive treatment of the topic.
[5] Irving E. Sigel, "The Piagetian System and the World of Education," *Studies in Cognitive Development: Essays in Honor of Jean Piaget,* David Elkind and John H. Flavell, eds. (New York: Oxford University Press, 1969), pp. 473, 486.

A major thrust of a teaching strategy is to confront the child with the illogical nature of his point of view. The reason for confrontation is that it is a necessary and sufficient requirement for cognitive growth. The shift from egocentric to sociocentric thought comes about through confrontation with the animate and inanimate environment. These forces impinge on the child, inducing disequilibrium. The child strives to reconcile the discrepancies and evolves new processes by which to adapt to the new situations . . .

•   •   •   •   •   •   •   •   •   •   •   •   •   •   •   •   •   •   •

Application of the Piagetian model to social studies depends on how the genetic epistomological model can be used . . . Thus, the social science curriculum builder may well find that the relevance of Piaget to his areas of concern lies more in the conception of mental operations than in the description of development in particular subject areas.

Similarly, Berlyne has concluded that in a wide range of cognitive activities, including concept formation, conflict must play a major role.[6] His work has reflected a variety of operational distinctions in levels of conflict or incongruity that suggest at least general applications to differentiated teaching strategies.

The traditional strategy of effecting concept learning through definitions has received a surprising amount of support in recent years. This simple approach involves a precise delineation of the critical attributes of the concept the teacher has, and then a transmission of this definition to students through written or oral forms, or both. Most of the self-appropriated learning that has taken place, so it would appear to some extent, has used this technique.

Such a technique, however, owes its success to a number of factors which generally cannot be assumed in the classroom, except for the learning of trivial concepts. These factors include: (a) students must have achieved a level of verbalization commensurate to that of the definer; (b) since the concept defined will involve other concepts prior to understanding it, such concepts must have already been learned by the students; and (c) the definition is self-explanatory, that is, raises no questions and demands no clarification for adequate understanding of it. It should also be remembered that students are frequently capable of identifying concepts without being able to define them accurately.

Some of the more crucial implications for the organization of curricular materials to facilitate concept learning concern (1) the degree of extraneous or irrelevant material, (2) the sequencing of exemplars, and (3) the variety in exemplars.

Degree of Extraneous or Irrelevant Material. In constructing or structuring materials for concept learning, teachers need to be exceedingly sensitive to the concept rule and its subsumed criterial attributes. These provide the focus for exemplars and nonexemplars and the parameters for relevant and irrelevant

[6] David E. Berlyne, *Structure and Direction in Thinking* (New York: Wiley, 1965), p. 247. See especially Chapter 9 on "Motivation of Directed Thinking: Conceptual Conflict," pp. 236–275.

material. To the extent that subject matter is not directly relevant to selected attributes, it may be said to be extraneous. Apart from the direct insertion, deletion, manipulation, or even fabrication of subject matter, teachers may emphasize only relevant material through such techniques as verbal cues (for example, statements or questions), written prompts, (for example, instructions or arrows), and learning sets (for example, immediate previous instruction in related concepts).

Sequencing of Exemplars. While a variety of variables appear to influence the selection of ratios and orders of positive and negative exemplars, both have a role in providing contrasts for a concept-learning task. Any illustration which is lacking in one or more critical attributes may be regarded as a nonexemplar; although for purposes of greatest contrast, it should lack all attributes.

With respect to the order of presentation, some evidence indicates that all exemplars and nonexemplars, clearly so labeled, should be made available to the student after their initial presentation. In this fashion, he may refer back to them, noting similarities and contrasts and generally reviewing salient features of the concept-learning task. This procedure contrasts with the frequent classroom pattern of introducing examples, removing them, and then introducing new illustrations.

Variety in Exemplars. The defining attributes of a concept appear to be learned more efficiently when a variety of varied and different illustrations is provided. In this situation a learner is permitted to develop inferences about commonalities, and hence about concept attributes, and then to test his generalizing in new situations. The minimum number of exemplars required, as well as the extent of the variety, will vary both with the complexity of the concept-learning task and the nature of the learner.

Other Considerations

Fancett *et al.* suggested that the teacher entertain four basic questions before initiating a concept teaching session:[7] (1) What prior concepts must the students know in order to cope with the new content? (2) What additional or new concepts are implicit in the proposed content? (3) Will the students be able to relate the newly acquired concepts "to important ideas" and "reach for important generalizations?" (4) What methods, techniques, and materials will most efficiently promote the learning of the new content?

Edith West has called attention to the importance of ascertaining the relative difficulty of concepts by considering certain conditions germane to the task.[8] She provides a chart (see Chart 1) to gauge the scale of difficulty of a concept in relation to selected criteria. While it does not provide definitive answers, it offers

---

[7] Verna S. Fancett *et al., Social Science Concepts and the Classroom* (Syracuse, New York: Social Studies Curriculum Center, 1968), p. 44.

[8] Edith West, "Concepts, Generalizations, and Theories," Background Paper #3," unpublished paper, Project Social Studies, University of Minnesota, no date, p. 6.

CHART 1. Difficulty of Concepts
(The listed criteria must be considered together, not separately)

Criteria of Difficulty	Scale of Difficulty: Easy	Scale of Difficulty: More Difficult	Scale of Difficulty: Very Difficult
Distance from child's experience	Within direct experience	Within vicarious experience	Unrelated to past direct or vicarious experience
Distance from observed referrents	Referrents are phenomena which can be perceived through senses Physical objects | Relationships (Specified | Defined Operationally) | Processes	Referrents are idealized types which do not exist in actuality	Referrents are phenomena which must be inferred from observations of other phenomena (constructs) Predispositions | Configurations | Processes
Scope of concepts	Narrow scope Few concepts subsumed under it | Relates few concepts	Broader scope	Very broad scope Many concepts subsumed under it | Relates many concepts
Certainty of presence of defining attributes	Always present		Tendency
Openendedness of concepts	Closed and so reliable	Not completely closed; somewhat unreliable	Open ended; vague boundaries; unreliable
Way in which attributes of concept are related	Conjunctive (joint presence of several attributes)	Disjunctive (presence of one or another attribute)	Relational Specified relationship (ratio, product, verbal) | Comparative | One attribute affects another | All attributes interact

SOURCE: Edith West, "Concepts, Generalizations, and Theories: Background Paper #3," unpublished paper, Project Social Studies, University of Minnesota, no date, p. 8.

some broad guidelines. West cautions that "although all of these factors are related to the difficulty of concepts, no one factor can be used as a satisfactory criterion."[9] She then offers these guidelines for developing curriculum:[10]

> First, curriculum builders must provide many direct and vicarious experiences for those concepts which are difficult. Second, the curriculum builder should limit the number of difficult concepts introduced within a brief period of time. Third, the curriculum builder must decide how many concepts of narrower scope must be understood prior to teaching a higher level concept which relates them. How many concepts must the pupil learn, for example, before he can be taught the concepts of "mountain pass," "harbor," or "region" in geography? Of "stratification" or "self" in sociology? Of "market" or "real income" in economics? Of "century" or "generation" in history? Of "interest group" or "constitution" in political science? Of "enculturation" or "modal personality" in anthropology? Finally, the curriculum builder must decide whether or not a difficult concept is significant enough to warrant teaching it in early grades when it might be taught more quickly at a higher grade level because of the types of experiences which most American children have had by the time they reach that grade.

Finally, she has developed a general index, indicated in Chart 2, to weigh the relative importance or significance of concepts.

OTHER VARIABLES INFLUENCING CONCEPT LEARNING

Teacher Versus Learner Conceptual Levels

For instructional settings, perhaps one of the greatest general variables in a concept-learning task is the degree to which there is disharmony between a teacher's and a learner's conceptual levels. Subconcepts or related concepts germane to a new concept-learning task are often held in different proportions by teachers and students. This phenomenon is quite likely to occur since both have probably constructed their related concepts from different experiences and networks of inferences.

Some of the more obvious instructional problems that may occur are that

1. the teacher realizes that there is a discrepancy between his and the students' conceptual levels and that some insight into his conceptual network is required.
2. the teacher discovers that he and the students use a similar symbol to denote different conceptual networks.
3. the teacher discovers that he and some of the students use different symbols to denote similar conceptual networks.
4. the teacher finds that inter- and intraclass levels of related concepts vary considerably.
5. the teacher realizes that some combination of the first four problems exists.

[9] *Ibid.*, p. 7.
[10] *Ibid.*

CHART 2. Importance or Significance of Concepts

Importance determined by following criteria:
 1. What is the scope of the concept? (i. e., . ^. many concepts are subsumed under it or related to it?)
 2. How many generalizations relate the concept ι her concepts?
 3. How significant are the generalizations which u. ιe concepts?
    (a) To what degree are they explanatory and preαictive?
    (b) Are they empirical generalizations, theoretical generalizations, or part of a narrow or broad gauge theory?

Scale of Significance		
Unimportant	Of More Importance	Of Great Importance
Limited scope	Broader scope	Very broad scope
Few generalizations using concept	A number of generalizations using concept	Many generalizations using concept
Generalizations using concept of little significance: (a) Nonexplanatory or predictive (b) Empirical	Generalizations using concept of some significance: (a) Explanatory (and probabilistic) (b) Theoretical	Generalizations using concept of great significance: (a) Explanatory and predictive (b) Part of a narrow or broad gauge theory

SOURCE: Edith West, "Concepts, Generalizations, and Theories: Background Paper #3," unpublished paper, Project Social Studies, University of Minnesota, no date, p.10.

In the first problem, a teacher must either focus upon helping students learn related concepts *prior to* proceeding to learn a new concept or restructure his approach to correspond to the students' conceptual networks. Similarly, in problem 2, the teacher must see beyond the trivial symbol similarity in communication patterns and work to restructure his approach. Problem 3, while it may result in much confusion, is the easiest one, since it involves only the learning of a new symbol—the conventionally accepted referent. Conversely, problem 4 presents the greatest challenge to a teacher and raises anew the fundamental question of individualized learning. Since each student's cumulative conceptual network is truly unique, it proceeds to assimilate and accommodate new data at both a rate and pattern equally unique. While it is quite likely that one's cultural context enforces in great measure a common configuration for encountering or perceiving data initially, the acquisition of conceptual networks appears to be highly individualistic and, hence, highly complex.

Even if a teacher had total knowledge of each student's conceptual network —a fantastic achievement—he would be unable to use such data efficiently to structure a concept-learning profile for each student. The mass of data involved would be too great to cope with, both as it relates to students' backgrounds and as it concerns the teacher's own, now expanding, concept of the concept he wishes to teach.

Factors Within the Learner

One of Piaget's most widely cited contributions to the development of instructional procedures in the elementary grades is his analysis of the stages of cognitive development in children. These stages, as indicated earlier, present a basic variable in concept learning by establishing the theory that children are normally best prepared to learn certain propositions at maturational levels that generally correspond to chronological ages. Children, for example, at the *concrete operational* stage that Piaget outlined must have concrete empirical props, illustrating the criterial attributes of the concept he is to learn, rather than purely verbal or abstract illustrations. Thus, concepts like "democracy," "government," and "legislature," while commonly found in curricula for children at the concrete operational stage, would normally be inappropriate to teach in their abstract form.

In this vein, it is important to reemphasize that children may learn a concept and yet be unable to verbalize it; that is, they may be able correctly to recognize, locate, and categorize instances of the concept without being able actually to state the rule of the concept.

It should be noted, too, that little empirical data exist concerning the scope and variety of concepts that students bring with them to school.[11] DeCecco has made this point succinctly, "As yet we have no studies of the concepts and principles with which most American children enter school and of the concepts they should learn first and those they should learn later."[12]

The unique emotional make-up of each individual student presents a highly significant, affective variable in concept-learning tasks. It is possible, in fact, that one's degree of affective involvement with a concept will overshadow and color his cognitive attachments. Carroll relates, for example, the case of the youngster who fears and rejects the barber because his white coat and scissors make him resemble the doctor, whom the child has learned to fear.[13] Carroll observes that "My concept of 'stone' may reflect, let us say, my positive delight in collecting new varieties of minerals, whereas your concept may reflect the fact that you had unpleasant experiences with stones—having them thrown at you in a riot, or finding lots of them in your garden."[14]

---

[11] See the following document for a listing of available studies: Irving Sigel and Elinor Waters, *Child Development and Social Science Education, Part III: Abstracts of Relevant Literature* (Lafayette, Indiana: Social Science Education Consortium, 1966).

[12] John P. DeCecco, *The Psychology of Learning and Instruction* (Englewood Cliffs, N.J.: Prentice-Hall, 1968), p. 400.

[13] John B. Carroll, "Words, Meanings and Concepts," *Harvard Educational Review*, XXXIV (Spring, 1964), 184.

[14] *Ibid.*

Nature of the Concept Itself

While some evidence does indicate the desirability of prominently featuring only criterial attributes in the development of concept illustrations, such a procedure is extremely difficult, if not impossible, for many social-science concepts. Normally, what occurs in the development of textual materials is that extraneous or noncriterial-attribute material is included in a concept illustration for the sake of developing and integrating a narrative. As an instructional sequence develops, coordinate and subconcepts are discussed, along with the featured concept; hence they may function as distractors or extraneous material and thus divert the learner from the intended concept. In a case study of the House Rules Committee, for example, the instructional objective may be to provide an illustration of the criterial attributes of the concept, "power." Through necessity, however, this case study is likely to include a variety of interesting but *distracting* details, including discussions of coordinate and subordinate concepts, such as "committee" and "chairman," since these facets are required to build the narrative. This problem of building extraneous material into instructional sequences also increases as the featured concept becomes more abstract, that is, as the network of related concepts necessary to discuss the featured concept increases in size and complexity.

Similarly, whether a concept is conjunctive, disjunctive, or relational will influence the ease with which it is learned. Conjunctive concepts (two or more attributes in common describe the concept) are easier to learn than disjunctive concepts (either one or the other of two or more attributes describes the concept) or relational concepts (a relation between two or more attributes describes the concept). Examples of these three types of concepts found in social-studies classes are: "power" (conjunctive)—the ability of a person or group to control another person or group and apply sanctions; "citizen" (disjunctive)—a person who was born in the United States, whose parents were born in the United States, or who has passed certain examinations;[15] and "waste" (relational)—that which is no longer of any use.

A learning task may become especially complex when a combination of abstract attributes, numerous attributes, and a nonconjunctive concept is involved. Using the legal concept of "tort," Carroll illustrates just such a combination.[16] "Tort" is outlined as having the attributes of (a) battery, (b) false imprisonment, (c) malicious prosecution, (d) trespass to land, (e) interference to chattels, (f) interference with advantageous relations, (g) misrepresentation, (h) defamation, (i) malicious intent, (j) negligence, (k) causal nexus, (l) consent, (m) privilege,

---

[15] Maurice P. Hunt and Lawrence E. Metcalf, *Teaching High School Social Studies: Problems in Reflective Thinking and Social Understanding,* 2d ed. (New York: Harper, 1968), p. 86.

[16] Carroll, *op. cit.,* pp. 198–199.

(n) reasonable risk by plaintiff, and (o) breach of contract.[17] The relationship of the numerous and abstract attributes, described by Carroll, is both conjunctive and disjunctive.[18] Some of the difficulties inherent in an instructional sequence for such a concept are reflected in Carroll's comment, "Presumably, a person presented with a properly organized series of positive and negative instances of torts could induce the concept, provided he also understood such prerequisite concepts as *battery, misrepresentation,* etc."[19]

Operating within a different frame of reference, Vygotsky provides another illustration of how the psychological differences between concepts may be viewed. His concern is directed at the developmental aspects of a youngster's conceptualizing, and he contrasts the growth of the concept of "brother" with that of social-science concepts.[20]

> Let us take the concept "brother" . . . and compare it with the concept "exploitation," to which the child is introduced in his social science classes. Is their development the same, or is it different? Does "exploitation" merely repeat the developmental course of "brother," or is it, psychologically, a concept of a different type? We submit that the two concepts must differ in their development as well as in their functioning and that these two variants of the process of concept formation must influence each other's evolution.
>
> •   •   •   •   •   •   •   •   •   •   •   •   •   •   •   •
>
> A child's everyday concept, such as "brother," is saturated with experience. Yet, when he is asked to solve an abstract problem about a brother's brother, as in Piaget's experiments, he becomes confused. On the other hand, though he can correctly answer questions about "slavery," "exploitation," or "civil war," these concepts are schematic and lack the rich content derived from personal experience. They are filled in gradually, in the course of further schoolwork and reading. One might say that the development of the child's spontaneous concepts proceeds upward, and the development of his scientific concepts downward, to a more elementary and concrete level. This is a consequence of the different ways in which the two kinds of concepts emerge. The inception of a spontaneous concept can usually be traced to a face-to-face meeting with a concrete situation, while a scientific concept involves from the first a "mediated" attitude toward its object.

CONCLUSION

One of the clearest implications for curriculum from the research literature appears to be that an organism does not necessarily recognize traditional discipline boundaries in organizing data for learning a concept. A youngster in the process of acquiring a concept of "president," for example, does not naturally limit his

[17] *Ibid.*

[18] For an extended clarifying analysis of this point, see DeCecco, *op. cit.,* p. 404.

[19] Carroll, *op. cit.,* p. 199.

[20] L. S. Vygotsky, *Thought and Language,* Eugenia Hanfmann and Gertrude Vakar, ed. and trans. (Cambridge, Mass.: M.I.T. Press, 1962), p. 87; p. 108.

cognitive search to the discipline of political science. As Carl Becker put the issue, "The normal and sensible man does not often drag the whole past of mankind into the present. But at any moment of deliberate and purposeful activity each one of us brings into present consciousness a certain part of the past, such actual or artificial memories of past events as may be necessary to orient us in our little world of endeavor.[21]

The key query to consider in curriculum construction then is "What is the most efficient and logical pattern for organizing data from the psychological perspective of the potential learner?"

SUGGESTED READINGS

Berlyne, David E. *Structure and Direction in Thinking*. New York: Wiley, 1965, Chap. 9.

Discusses succinctly how conceptual conflict may be used as a strategy to generate and focus thinking. Implications may be drawn for classroom instruction.

DeCecco, John P. *The Psychology of Learning and Instruction*. Englewood Cliffs, N.J.: Prentice-Hall, 1968, Chap. 10.

Lucid, well-written analysis of relevant research findings concerning concept learning, with suggested applications to classroom instruction.

Fancett, Verna S., *et al. Social Science Concepts and the Classroom*. Syracuse, N.Y.: Social Studies Curriculum Center, 1968.

A short general overview of selected literature relating to instructional procedures and issues concerning social-science concept learning.

Hunt, Maurice P., and Lawrence E. Metcalf, *Teaching High School Studies: Problems in Reflective Thinking and Social Understanding*. New York: Harper, 1968, Chaps. 4 and 5.

Excellent, brief discussions of the distinctions in instructional procedures for teaching concepts and for generalizations.

Shulman, Lee S., and Evan R. Keislar, eds. *Learning by Discovery: A Critical Appraisal*. Chicago: Rand McNally, 1966.

Perhaps the best one-volume critique of the reality, mystique, and unanswered questions attendant to discovery or inductive learning.

West, Edith, "Concepts, Generalizations, and Theories: Background Paper # 3." Unpublished paper, Project Social Studies, University of Minnesota, no date.

Perhaps the only theoretical discussion by a major social-studies project of the distinctions between concepts and other cognitive processes, and their implications for classroom instruction.

---

[21] Carl L. Becker, *The Heavenly City of the Eighteenth-Century Philosophers* (New Haven, Conn.: Yale University Press, 1932), p. 120.

part THREE

Instructional Models for Concept Learning

CHAPTER 6

Models for Structuring
Concept Learning

The philosopher May Brodbeck has written, "The term 'model' appears with increasing frequency in recent social-science literature. We encounter models of learning, of rational choice, of communication, of political behavior, of group-interaction, and so on, and so on. The term has moreover a decided halo effect. Models are Good Things."[1]

Parsons and Shaftel, too, have commented upon how widespread has become the use of models in curriculum work.[2]

> The development of models has become such a major part of current educational thinking that many large curriculum projects have defined this as their primary purpose. In one large school system of the Southeast, for example, the major curriculum effort of the past year has been the development of an "integrated model" for instruction. In this case the model itself has become disassociated from the phenomena which it was supposed to represent and the district staff has substituted working with the model for working with reality. Great amounts of physical and psychic energy and huge sums of money are being spent on developing the model while little serious attention is being given to its relevance to what is occurring in the schools.

Implicitly or explicitly, models are widely used in social-studies instruction and take on a variety of different forms in the classroom. Maps and globes provide a simple illustration of a situation where first two-dimensional and then three-dimensional objects are used to represent the earth. Similarly, simulation games as models provide a measure of correspondence between a competitive game-like situation and reality. More explicitly, teachers frequently put forth theory X or schema Y as "models" of how phenomenon Z operates in reality.

[1] May Brodbeck, "Models, Meanings and Theories," *Readings in the Philosophy of the Social Science,* May Brodbeck, ed. (New York: Macmillan, 1968), p. 579.

[2] Theodore W. Parsons and Fannie R. Shaftel, "Thinking and Inquiry: Some Critical Issues," *Effective Thinking in the Social Studies, 37th Yearbook,* Jean Fair and Fannie R. Shaftel, eds. (Washington, D.C.: National Council for the Social Studies, 1967), p. 141.

In commenting upon the importance of models, Marc Belth has observed:[3]

> Not only are we dependent upon the specific models we have available
> for the detailed interpretations, explanations, descriptions, and definitions of
> the data we encounter, but the logic of our thinking, the range of expectations,
> the anticipation and acceptability of sequence and the determination of dis-
> continuity are dependent upon the forms of the models we most frequently
> use.

TYPES OF MODELS

When a model and its representation share a close one-to-one correspondence
in many details, the model may be said to be *isomorphic*.[4] A minature train,
constructed to scale in every dimension, provides an illustration of an isomorph-
ism.[5] In the same way, Brodbeck suggests that *theories* whose laws have the same
form or are structurally similar can be seen as isomorphic and may be considered a model for each other. She offers the illustration of how the human
brain is frequently compared to an electronic computer.

Kaplan has distinguished five different senses in which the term "model"
is used:[6] (1) any theory stated in logically more rigorous or more mathematical
sense than is found in normal parlance (e.g. Rostow's theories of economic development); (2) a semantical model analogous to some data (e.g. "war on
poverty"); (3) a physical model corresponding to reality (e.g. a globe); (4) a
formal model which is a model *of* a theory (e.g Euclidean geometry); and (5)
an interpretive model which provides an interpretation for a formal theory (e.g.
computer simulation of human information processing).

Parsons and Shaftel have distinguished between what they regard as
categorical and *strategic* models in social studies curricula.[7] The former term
refers to those models usually developed at the end of an inquiry process to explain the transaction. Strategic models, on the other hand, are those which
provide a schematic illustration of a sequence of steps or processes. They offer
Crabtree's "Model of Geographic Inquiry" and Taba's "Three Cognitive Tasks"
as examples of categorical and strategic models, respectively.

VALUE OF MODELS

One of the chief values of models lies in their ability to predict reality with
a minimum of distortion. This facet of models allows their use in situations

---

[3] Marc Belth, "The Study of Education as the Study of Models," *The Social Studies: Structure, Models and Strategies,* Martin Feldman and Eli Seifman, eds. (Englewood Cliffs, N.J.: Prentice-Hall, 1969), p. 174.

[4] Brodbeck, *op. cit.,* p. 583.

[5] *Ibid.,* pp. 579–580.

[6] Abraham Kaplan, *The Conduct of Inquiry* (Scranton, Pa.: Chandler, 1964), pp. 267–268.

[7] Parsons and Shaftel, *op. cit.,* pp. 141–145.

where the employment of real objects would be impractical, expensive, or impossible. The prediction of voting returns on the basis of sampling models and the use of mock sites and materials to train moon-bound astronauts illustrates this point.

A related advantage of models is their explanatory dimension or their ability to simplify reality with a minimum of distortion. A simple illustration would be maps and globes; the Dewey five-step analysis of the key features in problem solving is another illustration. One of the better media illustrations of these dimensions of a model is provided in the film, "Model Man," designed for use within the "Econ 12" social studies. Focusing upon the concept of model, the film establishes clearly, in fewer than twenty minutes, an instructional sequence that facilitates the learning of the concept "model."[8]

While models provide a variety of useful functions, certain precautions concerning their use should be underscored. Belth reminds us, for example, that "Although anything that we encounter can be used *as* a model, nothing in and of itself *is* a model. Models . . . are constructed for the purpose of enabling us to think about the world experienced."[9] And the further removed a model becomes from the reality of its representation, the greater the danger that a slavish reliance upon it will result in a distorted view of reality.

Kaplan outlined six shortcomings of models of which users should be aware:[10] (1) overemphasis on symbols—the symbolic style may not *actually* specify the way in which terms actually are used; (2) overemphasis on form—concern with development of models may hinder direct progress in dealing with reality; (3) oversimplification—models are often simpler than the subject matter they represent; (4) overemphasis on rigor—models are often improperly exact and call for measures that cannot be obtained as specified; (5) map reading—the failure to realize that the model is just a "mode of representation, so that not all its features correspond to some characteristic of its subject-matter"; (6) pictorial realism—forgetting that a likeness between an object and a model exists only in a given perspective, that a model is not a literal statement. Kaplan concludes: "The dangers are not in working with models, but in working with too few, and those too much alike, and above all, in belittling any efforts to work with anything else."[11]

Brodbeck also cautions that "uncertainty, selection, idealization, and quantification are characteristic to a greater or lesser degree of most worthwhile theories."[12] She specifically warns against (1) speculation theories for which little concrete evidence exists, (2) the abstraction process involved in theorizing which tends to eliminate key variables extraneous to the theory, (3) the tendency to

---

8 Film is available through the Joint Council on Economic Education.
9 Belth, *op. cit.*, p. 174.
10 Kaplan, *op. cit.*, pp. 277–288.
11 *Ibid.*, p. 293.
12 Brodbeck, *op. cit.*, p. 587.

idealize in abstraction by reference to conceivable but nonexistent constructs, and (4) the propensity to quantify and misrepresent their significance. Examples of these four cases in the area of social studies might be: (1) man has a territorial instinct; (2) in capitalism, industries have as their goal the maximization of profits; (3) a total or complete free-enterprise system; and (4) correlation analysis in geography. In the first case, some empirical evidence exists but its import is not overwhelming. The second presents a generalization that is partly accurate but incomplete and misleading. The third suggests a conceivable ideal construct but one that has never existed nor is ever likely to in a social system. While the fourth indicates a highly sophisticated mathematical-statistical procedure for determining correlations between variables, it proves no causal relationships and may even correlate coincidental and insignificant factors.

Parsons and Shaftel suggest similar cautionary considerations related to the use of models. Their arguments relate to the possibilities that models may limit reflection by providing hasty closure and that they may become ritualistic procedures pursued as ends rather than means.[13] In their criticisms of a grade-one unit on Japan they provide an illustration of how misused models may seriously distort rather than facilitate instruction. Of the units' mode of organizing information, they state:[14]

> The food, clothing, shelter, school, and holiday scheme for organizing the unit information and sequencing the activities of instruction will have the unfortunate result of structuring a categorical model which children can internalize and use as the basis for subsequent culture studies. The difficulty of breaking out of this model once it develops is evidenced by the facts that children in all grades habitually approach culture study this way now, and that their teachers continue to limit themselves to these same narrow categories. From a strictly anthropological point of view, the major problem with this model is that it is an inappropriate and insufficient model for cross-cultural study for both children and adults because it considers neither the cultural determinants of, nor the more significant aspects of, human behavior.
>
> In addition to structuring too early cognitive closure, this unit raises the strong likelihood of ethno-centric reinforcement, itself a form of cognitive closure or rigidity. The major categories (food, clothing, shelter, family, holidays, and school) and the subcategories (occupation, cleanliness, and so on) are projections of the principal value foci in American culture. By using these particular categories to structure their information about Japanese culture, the unit calls the children's attention to the importance of these factors in life and provides them with opportunity for evaluating Japanese culture by comparing it with their own culture. Such comparisons invariably seem to be in favor of American culture, perhaps because of the nature of the categories of comparison.

[13] Parsons and Shaftel, *op. cit.,* pp. 141–147.
[14] *Ibid.,* p. 155.

SELECTED MODELS OF CONCEPT LEARNING

With these cautions and reservations in mind concerning the use of models as guides to instruction, several selected models of concept learning will be presented to provide guidelines for organizing subject matter more efficiently. These should offer the reader a variety of different schema that purport to predict or explain how the process of learning a social-science concept occurs. The models vary both in terms of specificity and in their origins. Some are diagrammatical, and some originate from social-studies educators, while others were developed by psychologists and related scholars. All generally share the common conception of a concept as a categorizing device with inference relationships, as suggested in an earlier chapter, but they differ in their interpretation of how these processes occur and in some other respects.

While the following models are outlined here as general guidelines, a subsequent chapter will *relate* these models to reality by providing an illustration of a concept-learning process predicated upon them and either drawn or inferred from their author's writings. Beyond suggesting how the models may actually be employed for structuring curriculum in preschool–secondary classrooms, these examples should allow the reader to gauge more carefully how the limitations and shortcomings of models are manifested in the transferral to reality.

A Piagetian-Based Model

This model is based upon those elements of Piagetian theory relating to the ability of children to deal with classification: to generate classes, to subdivide classes, and to reorganize classes on different bases. The clearest and most well-developed exposition of this model has been sketched by Irving Sigel,[15] and we will draw upon his work for our basic material.

During the period of "concrete operations" a child normally is limited to dealing with concepts that have empirical referents in some dimension of their structure, so that kindergarten and first-grade students, for example, tend to be more literal-minded. Children in this period will learn to develop the ability to add, multiply, divide, compare, or enlarge classes or categories. Items, persons, events, memories, etc. are grouped and sorted according to their attributes. Categorization may be predicated on the basis of a variety of different criteria including size, smell, shape, texture, hue, site, composition, function, or sound.

Concerning primary youngsters' ability to classify, Sigel remarks:[16]

---

[15] Irving Sigel, *Child Development and Social Science Education. Part IV: A Teaching Strategy Derived from Some Piagetian Concepts* (Lafayette, Ind.: Social Science Education Consortium, 1966).

[16] *Ibid.,* p. 2.

The awareness that items have many dimensions is a necessary first step in the acquisition of the knowledge that class membership is relative. *Classes, then, are formed and reformed on the basis of single attributes* [italics added]. Later children learn to build classes on the basis of two or more attributes. The ability to use two discrete attributes simultaneously as the basis for classification is a difficult process and one that children customarily *are not able to do until the fourth grade* [italics added].

Sigel qualifies this generalization, however, to permit the possibility that under appropriate instructional settings and with certain concepts, kindergarten and first-grade youngsters may acquire the ability of multiple classification. He found, for example, that material which could be presented visibly to children in three-dimensional form elicited multiple-classification tendencies. From this experience he concludes:[17]

> This would suggest that procedures to broaden styles of categorization could be instituted in the primary grades. Content would have to be selected which could visibly present to the child the possible alternative classification responses; later, use could be made of more symbolic representational material, such as pictures; and eventually, words.

According to Piaget, when a youngster is able to master multiple classes, he is able to grasp the important principle of conservation—the phenomenon whereby an item may be transformed and yet retain its initial basic characteristics. At this stage of development, children normally also acquire the capability of performing the mental operations of reversability and reciprocity which are prerequisite to the ability to deal with multiple classes; the latter construct includes the ability to deal with *relational* concepts and the former includes the capacity to see items as reorganized or reconstructed to their original state. Sigel found that children who were capable of multiple classifications were better able to learn a task through "a discovery-type approach, guided by the teacher," than through other approaches.[18] The sequence of considerations involved in the organization of a concept-learning task, according to Sigel,[19] is summarized in Table 1.

Taba's Model

Hilda Taba and her associates, like Sigel, also drew upon Piaget's work in developing their model of a concept-learning task. That dimension of their work that is directly relevant to our concern suggests a three-step cycle of experiences for developing a concept.[20] In the first step, frequent opportunities are provided for an analysis of sample, concrete exemplars of the concept. Students engage in

---

[17] *Ibid.*, p. 18.
[18] *Ibid.*, p. 14.
[19] *Ibid.*, p. 15.
[20] Hilda Taba, Samuel Levine, and Freeman Elzey, *Thinking in Elementary School Children,* Cooperative Research Project No. 1574 (Washington, D.C.: U.S. Office of Education), 1964, p. 49.

TABLE 1
SIGEL's MODEL

Considerations for Organizing a Concept-Learning Task

1. Objects, persons and events have many discrete attriubtes.
2. These attributes, individually or in clusters, can be used as the bases for forming classifications and, hence, for organizing content for a concept-learning task.
3. Classifications on the basis of an individual attribute is easier for students than classification on the basis of multiple attributes. For younger children, therefore, single-attribute items are easier to deal with.
4. With an appropriate instructional sequence and demonstrations, children can learn that individual attributes can be clustered to generate new subclasses through the combination of two or more attributes.
5. The intellectual operations of reciprocity and reversibility are cognitive prerequisites for multiple classification.
6. When students have acquired the operations of reciprocity and reversibility and are capable of multiple classifications, they are capable of conservation.
7. The use of discovery or inductive procedures can expedite students integration or coordination of attributes.

three types of activities in sequential order: enumeration of items; grouping of common items; and development of categories and names for the items.

During the second stage, analyses are then followed by tasks that "help the students to perform consciously that which they at first only did intuitively." Students engage in three types of activities sequentially: identifying points; explaining identified items of information; and making inferences or generalizations. Finally, there is a stage with experiences that call for the application of the concept to new events. This three-step sequence of tasks has been labeled "concept formation," "interpretation of data," and "application of principles," as illustrated in Chart 1.[21]

Gagné's Model

Gagné's work, as reported earlier, revealed the existence of eight distinguishable types of learning, each with correspondingly different conditions necessary to bring them about. As Gagné states:[22]

> To the person who is interested in knowing what principles of learning apply to education, my reply is: The question must be asked and answered with consideration of what kind of capability is being learned. The answer is different depending on the particular class of performance change that is the focus of interest. There are no "general" rules of learning known at present that can be used as guides in designing instruction.

[21] Hilda Taba, *Teaching Strategies and Cognitive Functioning in Elementary School Children,* Cooperative Research Project No. 2404 (Washington, D.C.: U.S. Office of Education), 1966, pp. 39, 40, and 42.

[22] Robert M. Gagné, *The Conditions of Learning* (New York: Holt, 1968), p. v.

CHART 1. Taba's Model

Concept Formation		
Overt Activity	Covert Mental Operation	Eliciting Question
1. Enumeration and listing	Differentiation	What did you see? hear? note?
2. Grouping	Identifying common properties; abstracting	What belongs together? On what criterion?
3. Labeling, categorizing, subsuming	Determining the hierarchial order of items. Super- and sub-ordination	How would you call these groups? What belongs under what?
Interpretation of Data		
Overt Activity	Covert Mental Operation	Eliciting Question
1. Identifying points	Differentiation	What did you note? see? find?
2. Explaining items of identified information	Relating points to each other. Determining cause and effect relationships	Why did so-and-so happen?
3. Making inferences	Going beyond what is given. Finding implications, extrapolating	What does this mean? What picture does it create in your mind? What would you conclude?
Application of Principles		
Overt Activity	Covert Mental Operation	Eliciting Question
1. Predicting consequences. Explaining unfamiliar phenomena. Hypothesizing	Analysing the nature of the problem or situation. Retrieving relevant knowledge	What would happen if . . . ?
2. Explaining, supporting the predictions and hypotheses	Determining the causal links leading	Why do you think this would happen?
3. Verifying the prediction	Using logical principles of factual knowledge to determine necessary and sufficient conditions	What would it take for so-and-so to be true or probably true?

These types of learning are arranged in a hierarchical arrangement, with all preceding types as prerequisites for higher-order types. Thus concept learning, Type six, subsumes five other types as prerequisites. The basic conditions specified for this type of task are sequenced in Table 2.[23]

[23] Robert M. Gagné, "The Learning of Concepts," *The School Review*, LXXIII (Autumn, 1965), 191.

TABLE 2
GAGNÉ'S MODEL

Conditions for a Concept-Learning Task

1. Show the subject an instance of the concept and specify its name.
2. Show the subject another and different exemplar (or several) and again specify the concept name.
3. Show the subject a *negative* instance of the concept and specify that it is *not* the concept name.
4. Show the subject still another positive exemplar and, pointing appropriately to the positive and negative examples, respectively, specify the concept name and specify that it is not the concept name.
5. As a test, give the subject a context and request that he illustrate or select the instance of the concept.

DeCecco's Model

This particular model by DeCecco was generated, in turn, by the basic model of teaching developed by Robert Glaser and presented in Figure 1.[24]

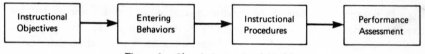

Figure 1. Glaser's Instructional Model.

DeCecco's model of concept teaching appears in his text, *The Psychology of Learning and Instruction: Educational Psychology,* and consists of nine steps.[25]

> Steps one and two pertain to instructional objectives. Step one requires a statement of the objective, and step two, a type of task analysis. Step two provides the student with the appropriate entering behavior. Steps three through six and step nine are specific instructional procedures for concept teaching. Steps seven and eight deal mainly with performance assessment.

These nine steps are listed in Table 3.[26]

In Step one the teacher defines the parameters he wishes to place upon concept learning by indicating what type of performance will be considered as satisfactory. DeCecco's model itself does *not* specify the dimensions of concept learning to be achieved.

In the following step, a teacher determines the number of attributes in the concept rule and arrives at a plan for highlighting critical attributes. "Two

[24] John P. DeCecco, *The Psychology of Learning and Instruction* (Englewood Cliffs, N.J.: Prentice-Hall, 1968), p. 11.
[25] *Ibid.,* p. 402.
[26] *Ibid.,* pp. 402–416.

TABLE 3

DeCecco's Model

Steps in Concept Teaching

Step 1. Describe the performance expected of the student after he has learned the concept.

Step 2. Reduce the number of attributes to be learned in complex concepts and make important attributes dominant.

Step 3. Provide the student with useful verbal mediators.

Step 4. Provide positive and negative examples of the concept.

Step 5. Present the examples in close succession or simultaneously.

Step 6. Present a new positive example of the concept and ask the student to identify it.

Step 7. Verify the student's learning of the concept.

Step 8. Require the student to define the concept.

Step 9. Provide occasions for student responses and the reinforcement of these responses.

general procedures," DeCecco indicates, "reduce the number of attributes of complex concepts: You can ignore some of the attributes and focus on those you think most important or you can code the attributes into fewer patterns."[27]

Step three is concerned with assuring that a student has the prerequisite verbal associations necessary for learning a new concept. To the extent that verbal associations have not been established a teacher must develop them before proceeding to Step four.

During this next step, students are introduced to positive and negative instances of the concept, sufficient in number to assure that all the critical attributes of the concept have been illustrated. Interestingly, DeCecco also notes that in this step "direct experience or realistic examples are usually not preferable to simplified presentations of the concepts, such as line drawings, cartoons, diagrams, and charts."[28]

In Step five, DeCecco recommends that examples be provided in close succession or simultaneously, with all exemplars available at all times for the student. In this way, he does not have to rely on memory for preceding examples.

Steps six, seven, and eight, respectively, deal with providing contiguity and reinforcement, assessing students' performance, and stating concept rules.

In the final step, further occasions should be provided to allow students to respond to examples and to receive appropriate reinforcement.

An Individualized Model of Computer-Assisted Instruction

Unlike the foregoing models, this one is intended to provide a learner with a pattern of content more closely geared to his past experiences, current motivational state, reading ability, and contextual preferences. In effect, the model

[27] *Ibid.*, p. 403.
[28] *Ibid.*, p. 412.

suggests a plan whereby a learner may begin a task at any given state of "conceptual readiness" (within set limitations) and proceed to learn a concept according to a variety of approaches from which he himself selects. This approach is *individualized* then to the extent that (1) the learner controls the operation, duration, and pacing of the instructional process, (2) the learner's past experiences and limitations are accounted for in the program, (3) some latitude is provided for shifts in the learner's motivational state, and (4) evaluation is available immediately to the learner at various intervals. Its features are outlined in Table 4.[29]

TABLE 4

AN INDIVIDUALIZED MODEL OF COMPUTER-ASSISTED INSTRUCTION

Sequence of Operations

1. Developmental Stage
   1.1 Develop or acquire testing instruments
   1.2 Select student population
   1.3 Pretesting
   1.4 Develop student profiles from pretests
   1.5 Organize data for interdisciplinary concepts selected and student profiles.
   1.6 Develop varied positive and negative instances of concepts in sequenced fashion.
   1.7 Develop questions concerning concepts
   1.8 Develop reviews for instructional sequences.

2. Programming Operations
   2.1 Introductory instructions for all students concerning use of the system.
   2.2 Correlate episode sequences with limited range of student profiles, plus develop additional alternative bank of varied positive and negative content episodes for students who wish to call them up.
      2.21 Upon identification, student is provided with a sequence of instruction based upon his profile.
      2.22 Allow for responses to provide direction for future routines.
      2.23 Make provisions for students requesting parallel or less complex or more complex examples by signalling at any point.
      2.24 Make provisions for students to request additional data during an instructional sequence. Such data would be called up by a "Key-Word in Context" (KWIC) sorting mechanism.
      2.25 Make proivsions for students to request print-outs for further exploration of data related to any episode which will be coordinated with individual profiles.
      2.26 Keep records of student interface with the computer.

Multidimensional Models

Attainment, Augmentation, and Demonstration Model. The following three models provide a broader focus than the others because they either deal separately

---

[29] For a discussion of the use of computers in the social studies, see Peter H. Martorella and Dixie Kohn, "Computer-Related Materials in the Social Studies/Social Sciences," *Social Education*, XXXIV (December, 1970).

with the discrete dimensions of concept learning or are concerned with the learning of a cluster of concepts rather than a single one.

In a chapter entitled "Teaching Concepts, Generalizations and Constructs," Tanck[30] takes the former approach. He considers three dimensions of concept learning, *attainment, augmentation,* and *demonstration*: attainment is regarded as the development of a basic understanding of a concept; augmentation is seen as the expansion of knowledge about a concept; and demonstration is regarded as the explanation, illustration, and comparison of examples and nonexamples of a concept. Tanck provides a model of these three processes which is summarized in Tables 5,[31] 6,[32] and 7.[33]

TABLE 5
CONCEPT-ATTAINMENT MODEL

Sequence of Operations

1. Identify the symbol, major attributes, examples, and nonexamples of the concept.
2. Present students with the examples, identified by their concept name, and with non-examples, and have them identify the critical attributes of the concept.
3. As an optional but desirable step, have the students define the concept by listing its major attributes.
4. Introduce more examples and nonexamples, and have students identify whether they are positive or negative instances and give reasons why or why not.
5. Have the students locate and label new examples.
6. Evaluate learning by ascertaining whether students can identify and can locate new ones.

TABLE 6
CONCEPT-AUGMENTATION MODEL

Sequence of Operations

1. Identify the concept symbol, attributes and examples already known, attributes and corresponding examples yet to be learned, and the nonexamples.
2. Have students compare examples with the new attributes and with those attributes and examples already known.
3. Include the new attributes in the concept's rule.
4. Provide practice in locating and classifying examples from new materials.
5. Evaluate learning of the new attributes and more complex examples by ascertaining whether students can identify examples and nonexamples and can locate new ones.

---

[30] Marlin L. Tanck, "Teaching Concepts, Generalizations, and Constructs," *Social Studies Curriculum Development: Prospects and Problems, 39th Yearbook,* Dorothy McClure Fraser, ed. (Washington, D.C.: National Council for the Social Studies, 1969).

[31] *Ibid.,* pp. 117–118.

[32] *Ibid.,* pp. 121–122.

[33] *Ibid.,* pp. 120–121.

TABLE 7
Concept-Demonstration Model

Sequence of Operations

1. Identify the symbol, major attributes, and examples and nonexamples of the concept.
2. Name and define the concept and note its major attributes. Optionally, it may be compared with other known concepts.
3. Provide examples and nonexamples of the concept through a variety of instructional formats. Initially, more examples than nonexamples should be used, and the examples should be simple and familiar. There should be progression to more complex and remote illustrations, with an increasing use of nonexamples. With the concept symbol prominently featured, the major attributes of examples and nonexamples should be illustrated.
4. Provide students with practice in selecting and creating examples of the concept.
5. Evaluate learning by ascertaining whether students can identify examples and nonexamples and can locate new ones.
6. Reinforce the concept periodically by repeating Step 4 above.

Conceptual System Model

Charlotte Crabtree's model, in contrast to Tanck's, is complex in two respects: it provides for the interrelated development of three concepts and generalizations within a single system, and it appears to be rooted in geographical inquiry rather than providing a general normative model. In analyzing the model, described in Figures 2[34] and 3,[35] therefore, the reader may have some difficulty in trying to generalize the model to other concepts.

Figure 3 provides some clarification for the various dimensions of the model. The model deserves special attention since it uses rigorous geographical data at the primary grade level.

ANALYSIS AND CONCLUSION

Models and model building, carefully delineated and viewed in proper perspective, can provide a teacher with a useful instructional tool. They provide a focus and a rationale for subsequent classroom behavior and allow generalizability which transcends a specific lesson or demonstration. Whether or not the teacher is cognizant of the fact, explicitly or implicitly to some degree, she uses models in the course of her instruction.

Several selected models of how a concept-learning process might be structured were offered to suggest some approaches for teachers to consider. While the

[34] Charlotte Crabtree, "Supporting Reflective Thinking in the Classroom," *Effective Thinking in the Social Studies, 37th Yearbook,* Jean Fair and Fannie R. Shaftel, eds. (Washington, D.C.: National Council for the Social Studies, 1967), p. 92.
[35] *Ibid.,* p. 94.

models all differ in varying degrees, they share certain fundamental commonalities.

Use of Exemplars and Nonexemplars. All the models, in some respect, emphasize the selection of data and organization of facts around exemplars of the concept rule and the use of nonexemplars as contrasts. The *most* structured

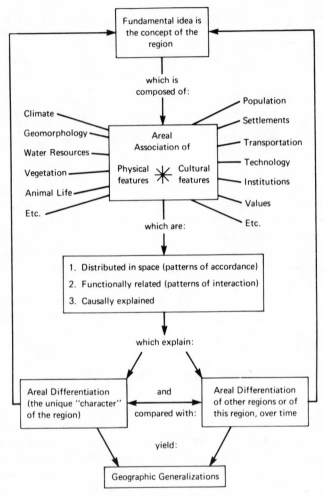

Figure 2. Crabtree's Model.

delineation of procedures for the use of exemplars can be found in the Gagné and DeCecco models; while the *least* structured approach is reflected in the Crabtree and Taba models. The function of concentrating upon exemplars and nonexamplars, of course, is to highlight what a particular concept is through iteration and contrast.

Systematic Instruction. A pattern that is clearly emerging in social-studies materials dealing with any dimension of cognitive processes is careful attention to the ways in which instructional processes are sequenced. This attention emerges in a variety of dimensions, ranging from specific alternative suggestions for how an instructional sequence might proceed toward a stated objective, as exemplified in the University of Minnesota, Project Social Studies materials, to highly structured individual lesson packages, as illustrated in the Carnegie-Mellon University, Project Social Studies, grades nine–twelve materials. The models for

Geographic Operation	Cognitive Processes Involved
1. Region is defined.	Data Gathering: Acquiring specific information concerning geographic features and their distributions within the region.
2. Forms or structures within the region are functionally analyzed. Cultural features are defined. Their functions analyzed. Their relationships examined. Hypotheses formed regarding patterns of associations within the region.	Involves: Acquiring knowledge of specific geograp features in the region. Acquiring knowledge of functions of specific cultural features in the landscape.
3. Spatial arrangements and patterns of interaction within the region are mapped and analysed. (Accordant relationships tested.)	Data Analysis: Organizing information and analysing in terms of patterns of distribution of features, as a means of testing hypotheses concerning the character and processes influencing this region. Involves: Applying concept of areal association in delineating functionally differentiated regions.
4. Systems of functional relationships between this region and other regions are examined.	Determining patterns of accordance in the distributions of features within the region.
5. Time sequence in the region, past and present, is examined. (Causal relationships tested.)	Determining causal relationships within the region as the consequence of changes through time.
6. Comparative regions are analysed, and generalizations formed.	Regional Interpretation and Theory Construction: Structuring, verifying, and evaluating geographic principles. Involves: Structuring revised statements of geographic principles or generalizations. Applying criteria of internal consistency and accuracy of the facts in verifying principles or generalizations.

Figure 3. Operations of Geographic Inquiry and Their Related Cognitive Processes.

concept learning reflect this general pattern and avoid the vague admonitions that pervaded many old teacher guides. Not only is the element of organization of instruction critical to the models, but the *sequence* of specific instructional moves and the absence of extraneous, distracting content are equally essential.

Sensitivity to Prior Knowledge. Traditionally, with the exception of a few bows to review of prior learnings and the reptition of topics, social-studies instruction has been insensitive to any notion of a cognitive structure of knowledge. Structuring content for concept learning, on the other hand, requires considerable attention to the knowledge base of students, since it presumes that the critical attributes of the concept rule are at least familiar to students. To the extent that they are not, students cannot proceed to learn the concept in question.

Practice Phenomenon. The models require a practice or exercise phenomenon in which the student tries his hand at manipulating and discriminating fact clusters in the process of learning a given concept. This practice or exercise phenomenon differs from rote verbal drills, homework association tasks, or review sessions in that they ask students to explore fact cluster relationships, to differentiate exemplars from nonexemplars, and to attempt creation of exemplars. Metaphorically, the student is requested to spin the web of a new cognitive structure and to assume some responsibility for selecting and organizing appropriate materials for the process.

Curriculum Organization. Traditionally, in social-studies curricula across the United States, the general pattern of organization has been according to the chronological sequence of events or the topical themes within a time slice. A cursory examination of the most frequently used textbooks confirms that these designs, with some variations, are still operative and dominant. The models for concept learning presented here, on the other hand, suggest that the structure and character of facts are more important in organizing instruction than their temporal placement or contextual identification. Whether facts interrelate as exemplars and are devoid of nonexemplars takes precedence over their chronological sequence or topical relationship.

In effect, then, the models imply a radical shift in the form of curriculum organization, with chronological and topical considerations given a less prominent focus. Instructional processes would proceed from concept nucleus to concept nucleus, with considerable variation in the actual subject matter based on the differences in backgrounds of the teacher and students.

Some illustrations of how subject-matter organization might occur according to the model is provided in subsequent chapters.

Evaluation. The need for evaluation is suggested in all the models, although not categorically specified in all cases. At a fundamental level, evaluation is always associated with the ability to distinguish accurately exemplars from nonexemplars. Similarly, some general diagnostic evaluation is presumed for the initial stage of facilitating concept learning in order to ascertain whether a student, as a prerequisite, has mastered the critical attributes in the given concept's rule.

SUGGESTED READINGS

Brodbeck, May. "Models, Meanings and Theories." *Readings in the Philosophy of the Social Sciences,* May Brodbeck ed., New York: Macmillan, 1968, Chap. 33.

A discussion of the nature, functions, and limitations of models.

Crabtree, Charlotte, "Supporting Reflective Thinking in the Classroom." *Effective Thinking in the Social Studies, 37th Yearbook,* Jean Fair and Fannie R. Shaftel, eds. Washington, D.C.: National Council for the Social Studies, 1967.

Presents a complex model for concept learning that involves a cognitive system.

DeCecco, John P. *The Psychology of Learning and Instruction.* Englewood Cliffs, N.J.: Prentice-Hall, 1968, Chap. 10.

Presents a nine-step model for concept learning along with succinct analysis of relevant research findings.

Gagné, Robert M. *The Conditions of Learning.* New York: Holt, 1965.

Presents a model for concept learning based upon the author's analysis of *eight* conditions for learning.

Kaplan, Abraham. *The Conduct of Inquiry.* Scranton, Pa.: Chandler, 1964, Part II.

An analysis of the nature, types, and functions of concepts from a philosophical viewpoint.

Parsons, Theodore W., and Fannie R. Shaftel. "Thinking and Inquiry: Some Critical Issues." *Effective Thinking in the Social Studies 37th Yearbook,* Jean Fair and Fannie R. Shaftel, eds. Washington, D.C.: National Council for the Social Studies, 1967.

Particularly thoughtful discussion of the limitations and possible deficiencies of models.

Sigel, Irving. *Child Development and Social Science Education. Part IV: A Teaching Strategy Derived from Piagetian Concepts.* Lafayette, Ind.: Social Science Education Consortium, 1966.

Sketches generally a model for concept learning that reflects Piaget's findings.

Taba, Hilda, *Teaching Strategies and Cognitive Functioning in Elementary School Children.* Cooperative Research Project No. 2404. Washington, D.C.: U.S. Office of Education, 1966.

This and the earlier project report presents an instructional model based upon three cognitive tasks with specific hierarchical procedures.

Tanck, Marlin L. "Teaching Concepts, Generalizations, and Constructs," *Social Studies Curriculum Development: Prospects and Problems, 39th Yearbook,* Dorothy Mc-Clure Fraser, ed. Washington, D.C.: National Council for the Social Studies, 1969.

Presents a three-phase model for concept learning that outlines procedures for teaching new concepts as well as augmenting old ones.

CHAPTER 7

Applying Models to Classroom Instruction in the Social Studies

An aspect of the utility of models is the fact that they transcend individual, isolated illustrations in a particular context and, hence, allow for varied applications. In this sense, instructional *models* allow for *teacher* individualization in a way that instructional examples do not. Imitations of *examples* in classroom instruction require the teacher to commit himself to a particular topic in terms of preparation and focus, whereas adherence to a *model* commits a teacher only to follow a structural pattern in interacting with whatever subject matter and focus he deems is within his competence and the legitimate purview of the class.

Nevertheless, while readers may need to concentrate upon abstracting models rather than specific examples, some illustrations of how the models may translate into subject matter for the social-studies classroom may be helpful. With this thought in mind, each of the selected models outlined in the preceding chapter have been applied to some level of social-studies instruction, preschool to high school. In most cases, where data are available, illustrations have been selected directly from the work of the model authors.

THE PIAGETIAN-BASED MODEL APPLIED

Sigel uses the illustration of a unit of study on the pioneers,[1] a topic commonly found in the curriculum, with the general objective being "to show something about the white man and the Indian in early colonial days." He suggests first the alternate development of the concepts of "tepee" and "log cabin" by (1) identifying their respective attributes, (2) discussing their respective functions as domiciles, their portability, their shapes, and the materials from which they were constructed, and (3) illustrating to students how these respective at-

---

[1] Irving Sigel, *Child Development and Social Science Education. Part IV: A Teaching Strategy Derived from Some Piagetian Concepts* (Lafayette, Ind.: Social Science Education Consortium, 1966), pp. 12–13.

tributes apply to the tepee and to the log cabin. At a second level, the similarities between tepee and log cabin would be discussed, such as those in their functions and materials. Then differences would be analyzed, such as those in their construction and shape. Having examined similarities and differences, students would be ready to examine these items and discuss or reflect upon the significance of each of their attributes.

Sigel suggests some typical questions that might be directed toward, for example, the attribute of shape: "Why is a tepee conical? What function does this shape serve? It is related to fire; a simple way to make smoke escape is to leave a hole in the top of a conical structure. Why is a log cabin rectangular? This is a simple way to build with logs."

Up to this point, the suggested procedures have focused upon how two discrete items may be shown to have similarities and differences, but with an emphasis on single attributes. Sigel notes that a teacher might now include in the discussion other types of dwellings prevalent in pioneer communities, such as lean-to's and clapboard houses, forts, and other types of buildings, "all of which have the common attributes of domicile, but which also have the other qualities which permit sub-classifications." A next step would be to locate in one category those buildings that were wooden and permanent domiciles and to place in another category those dwellings that were portable.

Sigel suggests that these procedures require students to discover the attributes relevant for discussion, along with their relationships.[2]

> From our research efforts it has become clear that letting the child provide the labels and discover the similarities and differences enables him to assimilate this information more readily, and to achieve an awareness of the complexity of items before him. This conclusion is consistent with the Piagetian theory, which holds that assimilation of information leads to alterations in the point of view. Thus, as these new bits of information become categorized in appropriate cognitive schemas, the schemas increase in content. The act of the child searching and labeling, uttering and hearing himself say "wood," "big," "small," and so forth, provides the context within which he acquires significant bits of information with which to identify environmental phenomena.

Discussion

The reader should note both the dissimilarity between the approach used by Sigel and that commonly found in units dealing with the "pioneers" and the extent to which he uses the topic only loosely as a guide to constructing an instructional sequence. His concern was only generally related to "pioneers," rather it was directed toward the more specific and more concrete peripheral concepts of "tepee" and "log cabin."

[2] *Ibid.,* pp. 13–14.

TABA'S MODEL APPLIED

Taba's multidimensional model also involved three states: concept formation; generalizing and inferring through interpretation of data; and application of principles. These stages or steps follow sequentially in developing the complete process of learning a concept. A series of edited tape transcripts of teacher-student dialog from a variety of elementary classrooms is included in Taba's study, *Teaching Strategies and Cognitive Functioning in Elementary School Children*,[3] and these will be used to illustrate the application of her model.

Concept Formation

The process of concept formation involves the cognitive operations of enumeration and listing, grouping, and labeling or categorizing; the transcript in Chart 1[4] indicates in part the operation of grouping.

CHART 1. Transcript of a Class Involved in Concept Formation: Cognitive Task 1

T	A, would it be all right if I put the letter A for all the things that go together with A? All right, let's begin/You want to start with the things that have to do with police? All right./Anne, why don't you start with that side and put a big A there on things that you think have to do with police/Does anyone else see any other items here which would come under another group. Another group. Carol, do you see another group?
Carol	Well, the architecture could be with the cities and the houses./They're all architecture.
T	I see. Would you like to put a B in front of all the things that you think go together? All right. As you wish, if you think it goes together, then while you are doing that we will read Anne's list./ Anne, you feel that all the things that go together would be, under A, would be different uniforms for policemen, police departments, not as many policemen, any others that you might have missed? Jimmy? Sam.
Sam	Lack of firearms could go with it./
T	You think that goes with policemen./ Is there anything else that you could, that you see, boys and girls, that might go under A, policemen, things having to do with police-men, John.
John	Wouldn't they be coming under, wouldn't they take their orders from government? They would be working under the government.
T	All right./You feel government is part of this group? O.K., can you show me where it is. John.
John	Right there (pointing to board).
T	You feel government is part of this group. Butch.
Butch	Wouldn't hospital come under uniforms? They wear uniforms, huh?
Several	Huh?

[3] Hilda Taba, *Teaching Strategies and Cognitive Functioning in Elementary Children*. Cooperative Research Project No. 2404 (Washington, D.C.: U.S. Office of Education, 1966).
[4] *Ibid.*, p. 151.

Generalizing and Inferring

Generalizing and inferring through the interpretation of data involves the elements of identifying points, explaining identified items of operations, and making inferences or generalizations. The transcript in Chart 2[5] suggests some of these operations.

CHART 2. Transcript of a Class Involved in Inferring and Generalizing: Cognitive Task 2

Dan	The country might not have enough money, to build a lot of schools — more schools than another country.
T	Okay. That's a very good reason.
Howard	Well, ah, in Brazil why they wear their uniforms in the rural areas is because they — these kids they don't have, you know, proper clothing or anything like this./ They just wear these little rags/ and so they give them these uniforms to wear to school.
T	And this is in the city?
Howard	No, this is in the rural areas.
T	Oh, in the rural areas, I see.
?	They have them in both.
T	Holly, you had your hand up. Can you think of some differences? I mean some reasons for these differences? Quality of education, the number of people going to school.
Holly	Well, maybe the ah, people didn't have enough money to buy the different things so they can't send their children to school./ They have to buy clothing and the children work.
T	So both you and Dan feel that money is one of the main reasons for the differences in the amount of schooling people get in different countries./ Can you think of other reasons?
Anne	They might need them to help their fathers in the field and other things more than to go to school and read and write./ They might not even need to write unless they were born in the city and have to work in factories./ If they were in the country they could just work in the fields and they really don't need to.
T	All right, I'm going to hold up right here for just a moment. And I'm going to have a few more of you, in fact . . .

Application of Principles

The third cognitive task, application of principles, subsumes the following processes: (1) predicting consequences, explaining unfamiliar phenomena, and hypothesizing; (2) explaining and supporting the predictions and hypotheses; and (3) verifying the predictions and hypotheses. These processes are reflected to some extent in the last transcript in Chart 3.[6]

[5] *Ibid.*, p. 153.
[6] *Ibid.*, p. 154.

CHART 3. Transcript of a Class Involved in Application of Principles: Cognitive Task 3

T   Okay. And when people move to other places what would some of the other things that would be likely to happen?

Harry   Well, they could — farmers may be could go back to cattle business/if they're at some other place.

T   Go back to cattle business — I didn't quite understand. Why would they raise cattle, do you think? If they couldn't sell any more beef?

Harry '   Well, if they moved to a different country or something/ and they raised beef, well, they know how to do it and —

T   I see. Oh, I see, they'd move to a completely different country that would be able to export it/. I see. Dick, let's talk a little bit more about jobs. Do you have any comments here about jobs?

Dick   Well, like Harry said, if they moved out,/well there would be less people to support./The government would have to support./And if enough people moved out/ like 20% would be from other crops/and they could start building up again.

T   I see. Are there any other side effects that you think might happen/when jobs become very scarce?/What are some of the other side effects that are likely to happen? Lou?

Lou   (no answer)

T   Suppose people couldn't get jobs any more./ Jobs became very scarce./ What are some of the other things that are likely to happen in Argentina? To most of the people? Doreen?

Doreen   Well, they would all get real poor they wouldn't have good homes./ And a few kids — children if they had education/ wouldn't get an education. And they wouldn't know how —

T   Okay. Loss of homes, decrease of education and Doreen carried that idea further . . .

Discussion

Unlike the other six models, Taba's, applied to classroom instruction, provides a multidimensional focus that goes beyond the learning and manipulation of a single concept. Moreover, Taba's work divides the cognitive process into three levels or tasks and establishes the relationship between these tasks and the importance of their sequential development.

Rather than isolate single concepts for development through all dimensions of learning, Taba's concern is initially for fundamental concept formation through enumeration, grouping, and labeling, then instructional movement proceeds toward involvement in concept-related cognitive operations.

Evaluation in Taba's model is accomplished through the use of a Social Studies Inference Test, An Application of Principles Test, a Sequential Tests of Educational Progress: Social Studies, and a Classroom Interaction Analysis System for categorizing student-teacher verbal behavior.

GAGNE'S MODEL APPLIED

To date, the application of Gagné's theories has been primarily in the areas of mathematics and science—one systematic application is the AAAS science series. Following his model, let us arbitrarily select a simple concept, "island," and sketch an illustration of how an instructional sequence might take shape.

Initially, a teacher would select a variety of positive examples of islands, as well as a variety of negative examples. The instructional procedure would commence with the teacher showing the students an example of island and specifying its name. As a second step students would be provided with another and different example of an island and again the concept name would be indicated. Students would then be supplied with a *negative* instance of island and the statement that it was *not* an island.

Comparisons would be made at the next stage by showing students another positive and another negative exemplar of island and specifying, in turn, that one *was* an island and one was *not* an island. To test youngsters' ability to discriminate correctly cases of island from noncases of island, the teacher would finally require students to illustrate or select instances of the concept. As required, then, the foregoing procedures would be repeated until students were able to discriminate at the criterion level required by the teacher.

Discussion

Since Gagné has narrowly distinguished the parameters of concept learning, his focus is limited to *discriminations* of exemplars. Other dimensions of the cognitive manipulations of concepts are reserved for his seventh and eighth types of learning, principle learning and problem solving respectively.

While he is not explicit on the point, it seems a fair inference that a teacher may be expected to discuss and even raise questions about examples of concepts and nonconcepts as she presents them to students. Less clear, however, is how Gagné would cope with the *extraneous* data normally included along with critical attributes in social-science concept examples.

DECECCO'S MODEL APPLIED

DeCecco provides an illustration of a teaching session dealing with the concept "tourist."[7] Using his nine-step process as a guide, we can illustrate each phase of the lesson.

[7] John P. DeCecco, *The Psychology of Learning and Instruction* (Englewood Cliffs, N.J.: Prentice-Hall, 1968), pp. 416–18.

Step 1. The teacher initiates the lesson by telling the class that she wishes to teach the concept of "tourist." She indicates further that students should be able to identify quickly examples of "tourist" at the close of the lesson.

Step 2. The teacher analyzes the concept and decides that it is a conjunctive concept with the critical attributes "activity," "purpose," and "residence." Related but noncritical attributes, such as "mode of travel," are rejected on the grounds that their introduction would confuse students.

Step 3. Students indicate the necessary verbal association by responding correctly to the word "tourist" written on the blackboard.

Steps 4 and 5. The teacher presents her positive and negative exemplars as verbal narrations written on large cards. Each card is left for examination after its presentation. Positive exemplars include vignettes, such as "Mr. Phog lives in San Francisco but he is on vacation and he is visiting Rome to see friends and the city." Negative exemplars are, for example, Americans who changed their residences to other countries. After presenting each exemplar the teacher waits for a response and indicates whether it is correct.

Step 6. Students are provided with a new positive exemplar—Mr. Angelo returning to Italy to visit friends and vacation.

Step 7. The teacher presents new positive and negative exemplars, varying national origins, regions, and purposes for travel.

Step 8. Students are required to write a definition of "tourist," which was composed against the teacher's original set of critical attributes.

Step 9. The teacher reinforces correct responses and indicates errors. Students are then reminded of the original objectives, given a test dealing with new positive and negative examples, and provided immediately with their results.

Discussion

In this illustration only defining and discriminating were required of students as evidence of concept learning. The teacher makes an important decision in Step two to distinguish certain attributes as critical and others as noncritical, and these divisions shape the character of her subject matter. It is useful to note that her subject matter, while having a basis in reality, is in fact contrived. Her concern for her objective in this case transcends any particular interest in, for example, accurate history.

One may also note that the procedures used in Steps four, five, and eight were possible largely because the students possessed certain verbal and maturational entry behaviors that young children would probably not possess.

THE MODEL FOR INDIVIDUALIZED CONCEPT LEARNING APPLIED

Applying the individualized model to a computer-assisted-instruction format would require curriculum development and programming stages.

Developmental Stage

In the initial stages, potential users of the instructional system would be pretested to develop individual "profiles." Profiles would include indices on such features as reading-ability levels, areas of particular interest, knowledge of subordinate and coordinate concepts, knowledge of critical attributes of the concept to be learned, and possible attitudinal orientations toward the general subject matter to be studied.

In turn, profiles would provide general indicators for constructing varied instructional episodes, including exemplars and nonexemplars of the concept to be learned, along with corresponding questions. The format of such episodes could also be varied: written (computer print-outs, computer instructions to consult short hand-outs adjacent to the computer terminal, or cathode-ray tube or television-screen messages); oral (tape or records); visual (computer-generated graphics, such as charts and graphs or simple drawings, still pictures, slides, films, or transparencies); or a combination of any of the preceding. A *basic* series of episodes for a narrow range of similar profiles might be constructed, and then additional *supplementary* episodes which might function in reviews and/or reinforcement or exploratory sessions could be supplied. Additionally, data relating to subordinate or coordinate concepts would be prepared and correlated with reading ability levels and interests for the students' retrieval, if they desired them.

Programming Operations

In the programming phase, provisions would be made for providing all users of the system with a common introduction to the use of the system, including its objectives, capabilities, and limitations. As students identify themselves to the computer, they would be equated with their profile indices and provided with the appropriate, individualized instructional sequence. Provisions would be included to allow students to switch to supplementary instructional series correlated with their profiles, if they should wish, or to request less difficult sequences, with respect to profile indices. In effect, when a student requests a less complex instructional sequence, he would be routed to another sequence based upon a profile with lower indicator scores, as the hypothetical rating in Figure 1 illustrates.

A Key Word in Context (KWIC) sorting mechanism would provide for retrieval of data relating to coordinate and subordinate concepts and correlated with some dimensions of the individual profiles. "Follow-up" work for students would be provided upon request, through references to sources that the student might consult. References would be based upon dimensions of the individual profiles and, perhaps, the rate of success in the computer-assisted instruction system.

Assumed Elements of a User's Profile

	Reading Ability Level	Knowledge of Critical Attributes Inventory	Knowledge of Subordinate and Coordinate Concepts Inventory	Interest Categories
User's profile index	9.1	1, 2, 4, 6	1.1, 8.3, 9.8, 11.5, 12.1, 12.4, 12.6	20, 23, 27,
Sequence provided initially	9.0	1, 2, 4, 6	1.1, 8.3, 9.8, 12.6	20, 23, 38
Some alternative instructional sequences (1)	8.5	1, 2, 3, 5	1.1, 11.5, 12.6	20, 23
(2)	8.5	3, 4, 5, 6	11.5, 12.1, 12.4	27, 29
(3)	9.0	1, 2, 3, 4, 5, 6	1.1	31, 38

Figure 1. A Hypothetical Case Illustrating a Computer-Assisted Instructional Sequence When a Less Difficult Sequence is Requested. The concept involved has six attributes, and difficulty is reduced by reevaluating and subsequently decreasing the assumptions made concerning a user's reading-ability level, knowledge of the concept's critical attributes, knowledge of subordinate and coordinate concepts, and interest areas. Correspondingly, the user is then provided with additional and/or different information than was supplied in the initial instructional sequence.

Finally, students would be evaluated in terms of their ability to: discriminate new exemplars from nonexemplars; differentiate the concept rule from a non-rule; and discriminate relevant attributes from nonrelevant attributes. Provisions would be made for keeping records of students' interfacing with the computer, and these would provide feedback for modification of the system.

Episode Sample

A brief, written sample of how an episode element from an instructional sequence dealing with the concept, "power," might appear as follows. This sample would normally be nested within the context of an introduction and a structural set on the learning task. It is correlated with a profile that indicates

a ninth-grade reading-level ability: knowledge of critical attributes, such as "control," "group," and "sanctions"; knowledge of coordinate and subordinate concepts, such as "monopolies," "politician," and "competition"; and an interest in such topics as "politics," "racial issues," and "businessmen." Negative exemplars have been omitted.

Sketch 1: An Illustration of Power. One of the main keys to competitive success in the nineteenth century was the controlling of prices. It was assumed that where businesses and factories were small, prices and output, along with wage and profits, rose and fell according to supply and demand and that every man was in equal competition with every other man.

Ordinarily, then, one's share of the market would be too small to permit any attempt at price control, unless he joined with others in a pool, a trade association, or another basic price-fixing agreement.

And in early nineteenth-century America this self-regulating mechanism did seem to work. Even after the Civil War, the individual businessman in the interests of self-preservation found himself forced, by and large, to observe the common rules of competition. In general, he avoided trade agreements for the practical consideration that such coalitions did not work since they were filled with mutual distrust.

What was true for individual businessmen and workers, however, was not the case for the giant corporation, which possessed greater unity of control and a larger share of the market, and was therefore in a strong position to dictate prices by engaging in monopolistic schemes. One example of the more effective combination of corporations is reflected in the newspaper clip which appeared in 1886: "Representatives of the various coal companies met at the house of J. Pierpont Morgan this week and informally decided to limit coal production and maintain prices." Thus, by collusion, which resulted in forcing the supply down and in maintaining prices at an artificial level not dictated by supply and demand, the major producers were able to make the public conform to their dictates because vital commodity was involved.

Perhaps a classic example of a solitary company dominating the market of a key commodity and hence being able to control its terms of trade and prices, is found in the history of the Standard Oil Company at the close of the nineteenth century. By a systematic process of securing rebates from the railroads, Rockefeller, the head of Standard Oil, was able to achieve a considerable advantage over competing oil producers, and thus to maintain a dominant position in the oil-refining industry. Eventually, by buying out or forcing out competitors, Rockefeller was able to control virtually all oil refining in the United States.

From domination of the refining business, he then was able to control oil prices throughout the country, even though Standard Oil itself *produced* only a small share of American petroleum. Similarly, the economic might of the company became so great that Rockefeller was able to force his product upon unwilling distributors by threatening to create competitive businesses overnight to drive them out.

Sketch 2: An Illustration of Power. In the period following World War I the Ku Klux Klan was able to build its membership up to between four and five million by 1925. The Klan had moved to the North and enrolled its greatest memberships in Ohio and Indiana. Its program included the "Christian religion," "white supremacy," the protection of womenhood, "pure Americanism," states' rights, the destruction of lawlessness and foreign agitators, and the limitation of foreign immigration, among other points. It desired more and better patriotism and set out to control church and state to achieve that end. It became involved with the contents of textbooks, entered political offices in many states, and took charge of public and private morals by floggings and displays of fiery crosses to bring "wrongdoers" back to the paths of virtue.

At its peak, it elected many public officials, including governors, Senators, Congressmen, judges, and numerous local politicians. Police and sheriffs were frequently controlled by the Klan. Klansmen, themselves, were told not to believe what they read in the papers for it was said that the American press was controlled by Jews, Catholics, and immigrants. Many tradesmen, small businessmen, and generally middle-class Americans who belonged to the Klan came to believe that Negroes and foreigners constituted a real threat to American institutions.

Religion and the schools came in for careful attention by the Klan. It made numerous visitations to Protestant churches, leaving behind copies of the Bible, flags, or even a money gift for the preacher. Decked out in hoods and sheets, the Klansmen found their church visitations to be good advertising for their organization. On the other hand, the parochial school was brought into conflict with the public school by the Klan. It called for a federal Department of Education with wide controls and for Bible-reading in the schools, prominent display of the American flag, and the expulsion of non-American influences from the schools.

In each state the Klan had a central headquarters, but these did not have much control over the local klaverns. In the small, rural towns and in the decaying areas of urban industrial neighborhoods, the local klaverns ruled themselves. They frequently made the decision to flog an errant soul or to intimidate with a cross-burning. Often they arranged to drive through "Niggertown," with hoods and weapons, in order to remind the blacks to "stay in their place" or face the consequences. Occasionally, Klan members were even used by industrial leaders in the South to frighten off labor organizers.

The Ku Klux Klan was able to satisfy the craving of many Americans for excitement and to provide an outlet for their pet hatreds. For thousands, its pageantry of robes and burning crosses and its acts of violence gave a sense of dignity and importance, although false, and a measure of control over those they hated and feared.

Sketch 3: An Illustration of Power. Virtually all bills in the House of Representatives must be routed through the Rules Committee after they have cleared the initial committee to which they were assigned. The Committee may then recommend, by attaching resolutions or rules to the bills, that the House take up certain bills for consideration. The rules specify, among other things, how much time will be allowed for debate and whether floor debate on the bills will be permitted. The original purpose of this screening process was to conserve the time and energy of Congress by eliminating nuisance or trivial bills.

If a majority of the Committee or its chairman desires, however, the legislative committee originally in charge of a bill can be made to revise it in order to receive a rule. In effect, by appropriate guidance, the Rules Committee can modify virtually any bill to suit *its* desires. At present fifteen men make up the Committee, and since only a majority vote is necessary to report out a bill for the House's consideration, eight men can control the fate of most bills in the House. The chairman of the Committee, too, like all Congressional chairman, can *himself* usually prevent a bill from receiving a rule merely by placing the bill very far down on the Committee's agenda or by refusing to convene the Committee when a particular bill is due for consideration.

A representative example of how the Committee can keep a key bill from the floor of the House, where its merits and defects could be discussed and where it could then be voted up or down, is the handling of the 1961 federal aid-to-education bill. Under the pretense that the education bill would be released when legislation to provide aid to parochial schools was given to the Rules Committee, the bill was held up in order to prevent debate and voting on the floor of the House. When the parochial aid bill arrived, however, still no action was taken. Eventually, in an 8–7 vote, the Committee decided to shelve all pending aid-to-education bills. The deciding vote was cast by a Committee member whose constituency was predominantly Catholic and therefore desirous of the bill's defeat. Not the House but the Rules Committee had decided against the desirability of the bill.

A few ways of circumventing the Rules Committee exist, but they are complex, cumbersome and require support from a considerable number of Congressmen. Furthermore, Congressmen are reluctant to bypass the Committee because they fear similar acts against the committees of which they are a member or because they are sensitive to future reprisals from a miffed and angered Rules Committee. The Committee may, for example, pigeonhole the Congressman's future bills or else attach crippling resolutions to them in order to prevent their passage. Finally, the Committee may brandish the weapon of refusing to kill those bills which a Congressman does *not* wish to have the opportunity to vote upon, since his constituency is sharply divided upon an issue and no matter how he votes he will alienate many people. This negative function of the Committee is often an important one to a politically insecure Congressman.

Discussion

While this model in application provides considerable individualization potential, the tasks involved in the preparation of instructional operations are considerable. What is required in developing such a system is a listing of the variety and parameters of constraints that one wishes to impose (for example, the range of differences that will be allowed in categorizing profiles, the variety and types of subject-matter outputs that will be used, the number of alternative instructional sequences that will be permitted, and the degree of sophistication in the pretests employed).

On the other hand, this model in practice would allow for a wider latitude of learning options than most schema for individualization that are operative today.

MULTIDIMENSIONAL MODELS APPLIED

Tanck's model, it will be recalled, suggested three possible dimensions to concept learning, each dealing with different but related tasks. As such, it provides for a more complex analysis of the general process of concept learning and allows one to consider three different cognitive conditions within a potential learner, although his model specifies no necessary sequential relationship between these conditions.

In the illustration of "concept attainment" Tanck is concerned with "associating related kinds of knowledge in context,"[8] whereas with his "concept demonstration" example, he is involved with an initial explanation of facts. Finally, with the illustration of "concept augmentation," he shows how new elements may be added to one's existing cognitive structure.

Concept Attainment Illustration[9]

Selecting the concepts of "land," "labor," and "capital," Tanck defines their attributes and suggests some contexts. Attributes are then associated with the concept symbol. Students studying about New England, for example, may read about lobster fishing and deep-sea fishing and then be shown pictures dealing with these activities, while being questioned about the major attributes. For example, a teacher may show a picture of a lobster trap, indicate that it is "capital," and ask, "Is this used in the fishing industry?"

Following these activities, nonexamples, such as pictures of children playing on a beach, are introduced and discussed. At the conclusion of the example and nonexample presentations, the concepts are defined by listing their attributes. Tanck suggests, "The teacher might simply ask students to tell what they think land, labor, or capital is or he may use a 'gimmick' like giving students cards with pairs of attributes on each and asking whether land, labor, capital, or none of these is described."[10]

Subsequently, additional exemplars and nonexemplars are presented in varied contexts, such as Pennsylvania coal mining and Florida fruit production, and students are asked whether specific incidents illustrate the three concepts and why.

In the next stage, students are required, through reading, sorting data, viewing films, and the like (concerning, for example, cotton cultivation), to find new examples of land, labor, and capital. Or they may be asked to *create* examples through stories.

As a concluding step, students are evaluated on their attainment by being asked to indicate whether a new set of pictures may be classified as either of the three concepts in question.

Concept Demonstration[11]

For this dimension of concept learning, Tanck uses the illustration of the concept, "culture." He suggests that initially the teacher should have the students read and discuss "a short written explanation" of culture. As a follow-

---

[8] Marlin L. Tanck, "Teaching Concepts, Generalizations and Constructs," *Social Studies Curriculum Development: Prospects and Problems, 39th Yearbook*, Dorothy McClure Fraser, ed. (Washington, D.C.: National Council for the Social Studies, 1969), p. 117.

[9] *Ibid.*, p. 117.

[10] *Ibid.*, p. 119.

[11] *Ibid.*, pp. 120–121.

up, the students are given lists of familiar objects and are instructed to discuss why one list characterizes elements of culture, while the other does not. The "cultural" list might include artifacts like houses, electric motors, and lawns, and the noncultural list could include swamps, lightning, and sparrows.

Subsequently, more complex examples are provided in new lists, and the preceding level of discussion is repeated. These lists might be reading, smoking, believing in democracy versus color of the skin, amount of body hair, and digestion.

Tanck suggests that students then be asked to list ten cultural and ten noncultural phenomena in the school neighborhood and to collect corresponding pictures. Evaluation is accomplished through an assignment whereby students are to sort given items into cultural and noncultural categories.

Reinforcement of these processes are to follow. Tanck recommends: "For example, as the students study ancient Egypt, they discuss which things influencing Egyptian life were cultural and which were natural. As they read in language arts, they sometimes discuss which portions of characters' environments and behaviors were cultural and which were not."[12]

Concept Augmentation[13]

Returning to the concept of "labor," Tanck uses as his data contexts the professions of doctor, teacher, clergyman, and the tourist industry. Augmentation of the concept revolves about the new attributes—labor is used in the production of services, and it may involve physical, mental, or emotional effort.

After reading about a doctor's work, for example, students might be asked:[14]

How is the doctor like the fisherman?
How is the doctor different from the fisherman?
Is the doctor labor?
Does the doctor produce goods, as the fisherman does?
Does the doctor work more with his muscles, brains, or feelings?

Related discussions could compare attributes of other professions, concluding with a discussion of how students can tell if someone is an example of labor or what labor is like.

Practice follows; student's work with subclasses designated by different attributes of labor, or collect pictures of examples of nonphysical work labor. Students might be shown pictures of workers, professional people, and non-laborers and then be asked to discriminate among the producers of goods,

---

[12] *Ibid.*, p. 121.
[13] *Ibid.*, pp. 121–23.
[14] *Ibid.*, p. 122.

the producers of services, those who do physical labor, those who do mental work, those who do emotional work, and the nonproducers.

Evaluation is accomplished through two methods: One is, for example, to describe a mother in various activities, such as paying bills, soothing a crying child, and sweeping the floor, and then to ask students to indicate whether she is or is not an example of labor. A second approach would be to read a story relating to a "community in another culture," and then request students to list all examples of labor. "If they include persons who produce services and who do mental and emotional work they are probably aware of the new attributes and the new types of examples."[15]

Discussion

The dimensions of attainment and demonstration, taken together, constitute the *minimal* concept-learning process with which most teachers will be concerned. Tanck's attainment dimension, taken singly, closely corresponds to Gagné's model applied to the classroom. The dimension of demonstration, in effect, provides for more practice in the use and application of a concept.

Augmentation appears to be an "enrichment" dimension of concept learning, in which a teacher attempts to systematically expand the existing well-formed conceptual network of students. While Tanck does not discuss the point, presumably this phase of concept learning is the least difficult of the three to facilitate, since it builds upon an established process. As an hypothesis to entertain, augmentation might be considered as the dimension most amenable to "home" work or to student-directed work in general, wherein students augment given concepts with little formal supervision or instructions.

CONCEPTUAL-SYSTEM MODEL APPLIED

Crabtree, by recounting her observations of a project, provides an example of the application of her model with children in grades one through three. She reports the ways in which questions were raised about how a city could meet its vastly expanding construction needs and about certain locational relationships in general.[16] Visits were made to new freeways under construction and a new mall nearing completion; new apartments, the city's public works programs, including street repairs, and rail facilities, where gravel rock products arrive daily, were also observed. Specifically, questions focused on the sources of the supply of gravel, cement, and concrete for the construction, since local resources in the community were nearly exhausted.

[15] *Ibid.,* p. 123.
[16] Charlotte Crabtree, "Supporting Reflective Thinking in the Classroom," *Effective Thinking in the Social Studies, 37th Yearbook,* Jean Fair and Fannie R. Shaftel, eds. (Washington, D.C.: National Council for the Social Studies, 1967), p. 95.

In the next stage, a terrain model was introduced representing the topography of the Los Angeles lowlands, the mountain rim, and the deserts to the north and southeast. Through the placement of small, red houses on the model, children were asked to indicate where they thought rock products might be found. Then, through data on the range, a soil box, and a simulation of water washing gravel down the mountains to the lowlands, students were able to evaluate their location hypotheses and then revise them.

At this point, an acetate overlay unit was used to indicate rivers, a map legend, and mining sites. Children then formulated statements about the relationship of sites to geographic features. Crabtree interprets: "At a 'concrete' level their statements incorporated relationships between granitic mountains, rock products, and the downhill flow of streams. At a more abstract level, their statements identified an areal relationship between the resource and the mining site."[17]

At the next level, the issue of whether the relationship between resource and mining site, if correct, was applicable to cement products was pursued. Through reading and charts, the students hypothesized sites for cement plants and tested their ideas by examining actual sites. They noted that actual location was based on factors broader than the strictly geographical ones that they had used.

Consequently, Crabtree states that, "Children reversed their earlier premise and claimed now, at an abstract level, that mining sites depended on both the location of the resource and settlements, market, and labor supply."[18]

Crabtree concludes the example dealing with the region of greater Los Angeles by referring to her model and noting that:[19]

> Children had . . . (1) identified certain facts concerning locations of physical and cultural features. They had (2) determined certain patterns of correspondence in the distribution of those features and verified those patterns against the data presented in the acetate overlays. They had, finally, by comparing two such systems of relationships, (3) induced and refined a geographical generalization, supported now, by considerable verifying evidence.

Discussion

As noted in the discussion of her model, Crabtree does not isolate a single concept for development, but rather deals with a cognitive network. In the illustration provided, for example, very little attention is actually devoted to assisting youngsters in learning a concept of regions, while a great deal of systematic, carefully formulated instruction is directed at the development of a sophisticated, tested generalization relating to regional interrelationships. To

[17] *Ibid.*, p. 96.
[18] *Ibid.*, p. 97.
[19] *Ibid.*, p. 98.

this extent, Crabtree's model and example deal more with the development of concept systems as a unitary process than with the development of discrete concepts and, subsequently, concept relationships.

CONCLUSION

The models developed in the preceding chapter were translated here into sample classroom illustrations to suggest their utility. To some extent, all the models, applied to classroom instruction, differ in both scope and characteristics. All, however, provide a basic component of what we refer to as "concept learning." To be sure, these models in their translation do not encompass the multiple, complex dimensions of facilitating the learning of *all* types of social-science concepts, nor do they reflect a common response over the issue of how sequential or clustered concepts should be taught.

What they *do* seem to provide is a more systematic and justifiable pattern for organizing subject matter toward an objective that all teachers of social studies ascribe to, but frequently seem unable to accomplish. To assume, as curriculum developers and practitioners so frequently have done, that the learning of concepts emanates systematically from the exposure to topically related facts is clearly unwarranted. There is, on the other hand, at least some empirical and considerable logical evidence to indicate that the paths charted by the models examined approximate more closely the most efficient routes to systematic concept learning.

SUGGESTED READINGS

Crabtree, Charlotte. "Supporting Reflective Thinking in the Classroom," *Effective Thinking in the Social Studies, 37th Yearbook,* Jean Fair and Fannie R. Shaftel, eds. Washington, D.C.: National Council for the Social Studies, 1967.

Presents an illustration from the primary grades of how a complex concept-learning model may be applied.

DeCecco, John P. *The Psychology of Learning and Instruction.* Englewood Cliffs, N.J.: Prentice-Hall, 1968, Chap. 10.

Provides an illustration of how a nine-step model for concept learning may be applied to the teaching of the concept "tourist."

Gagné, Robert M. *The Conditions of Learning.* New York: Holt, 1965.

Applies the author's models for the eight conditions of learning to the subject areas of mathematics and science.

Sigel, Irving. *Child Development and Social Science Education. Part IV: A Teaching Strategy Derived from Some Piagetian Concepts.* Lafayette, Ind.: Social Science Education Consortium, 1966.

Suggests some possible applications of selected aspects of Piaget's work.

Taba, Hilda, *Teaching Strategies and Cognitive Functioning in Elementary School Children*. Cooperative Research Project No. 2404. Washington, D.C.: U.S. Office of Education, 1966.

This and the earlier project report present sample classroom materials, evaluation procedures, and transcripts of classroom dialog relative to the three cognitive tasks.

Tanck, Marlin L. "Teaching Concepts, Generalizations, and Constructs." *Social Studies Curriculum Development: Prospects and Problems, 39th Yearbook*, Dorothy Mc-Clure Fraser, ed. Washington, D.C.: National Council for the Social Studies, 1969.

Provides illustrations of the three-phase model for concept learning with varied social-studies material.

part **FOUR**

Guidelines for
Curricular Change

CHAPTER 8

Concept-Learning Exercises

At this point the reader may find it useful to engage in some exercises relating to various dimensions of concept learning. Through actual involvement in some of the cognitive processes associated with concept learning, it may be possible to see more readily the meaning and significance of the conclusions reported in earlier chapters and to better apply them to instructional strategies.

Much has been written in recent years about the necessity to train teachers through the *same* techniques and strategies that they will use in teaching elementary and secondary students. This vein of argument advances, for example, that if teachers are to use "inductive" or "discovery" teaching procedures, they, themselves, must be taught by the inductive or discovery approach. The argument frequently continues to the conclusion that courses specifically dealing with "methodology" should be *models* of how to teach.

There is a powerful lure to this notion, particularly when entertained against the backdrop of current student protests over the quality and character of college and university teaching. Furthermore, the "mirror-effect" procedure of reflecting in practice what one recommends that others do helps to establish the professional credibility of the instructor in the eyes of his students. These factors notwithstanding, however, the idea that teachers should be *taught* by the same procedures that they will use in *their* classrooms with elementary and secondary youngsters remains a working hypothesis to be empirically validated. There may well be sufficient evidence for this position, but as yet the empirical evidence has not been collected.

THE SCOPE OF THE EXERCISES

In presenting these exercises, an alternative thesis is offered, namely, that all organisms require some *model* upon which to predicate subsequent behavior. Such a model may be abstracted from the behavioral specimens of a teacher *actually engaged in teaching one about a model;* it may be derived from a set of instructions concerning the model; it may be acquired from the analysis of behavioral specimens; or it may evolve from reflecting upon one's actions in a situation.

To illustrate, a model of how to teach a concept might be abstracted by a teacher from any of these four experiences:

1. Teachers are taught a concept by another teacher through a series of systematic procedures.
2. Teachers read a treatise, such as this book, on how to teach a concept.
3. Teachers may analyze behavioral specimens of other teachers teaching a concept under real or simulated classroom conditions.
4. Teachers may teach a concept by following a set of procedures and later analyze their own behavior specimens and the subsequent effects on students.

All four situations provide a basis for potential model-generating and may be used to reinforce one another, as occasionally happens in teacher-education programs. *All things being equal,* when the *sole* objective is to provide a model of how to teach a concept, it is difficult to argue for the relative superiority of any one of the four approaches.

Combinations of the orientation of the first, second, and fourth approaches are used in the five exercises that follow. In addition, a transcript of a kindergarten class exercise is provided in the Appendix, thereby offering the teacher a behavior specimen for analysis, as suggested in the third approach.

The exercises are designed to acquaint the reader through direct involvement with some of the dimensions involved in preparing students for a complete concept-learning task and also with how progress may be gauged. Provided are basic procedures, opportunities for analysis of one's own behavior specimens as he proceeds through the exercises, and methods of determining and comparing progress. It is suggested that the reader follow these steps in completing the exercises: (1) perform the exercises; (2) analyze the cognitive processes that were taking place during the exercise; (3) analyze the objectives of the exercise; (4) draw conclusions concerning the value of the exercise, and (5) consult the Appendix at the end of this book for answers (where applicable) and comparative comments on the exercises.

A CATEGORIZING GAME

This game is called "Would You Like to Be . . . ," which any number can play. There are no "winners" or "losers" as such, but one may be considered successful if he is able to respond and unsuccessful if he fails to answer. If played with a group, one member acts as a leader and asks each person, in turn, the questions. When the game is played by only one person, he answers all the questions. In either event, the game proceeds until the questions are exhausted. Analysis then follows.

Game Rules

1. You may not respond to questions with just a "yes" or "no."
2. In responding, your answer must be in the form "(Yes) (No), I (would) (would not) like to be ———."
3. You may not *complete* your response by using the same word(s) as the one(s) used in the questions.
4. Questions must be in the form "Would you like to be (a) (an) ———?"
   Example: "Would you like to be a carrot?"
   Answer: "No, I would not like to be a vegetable."

Sample Questions

"Would you like to be (a) (an) ———?" (banana, dog, car, chair, suit, hammer, door, shoe, river, television set, house, forest, soldier, enemy, army, rule, economy, colony, government, nation, century, theory). Sample lists for use with young children and with older students are provided in the Appendix.

Discussion

The foregoing game was devised by a three-year-old and has been played, using different sets of items, with groups ranging from preschool children to graduate school students. While simplistic in structure, it has considerable potential for illustrating different dimensions of concept-learning tasks to groups with diverse cognitive sophistication.

AN INFERENCE EXERCISE

The ability to generate an inference involves going beyond data immediately present in a situation to draw a conclusion that appears likely. For example, I look at the sky and observe dark clouds, from which I conclude that it will rain. A classical illustration of inference is Sherlock Holmes, who consistently goes well beyond the data at his disposal to draw "elementary" conclusions, much to the amazement of his colleague, Dr. Watson.

In concept learning, inferences play a key role in allowing a person to establish a class identity for a set of observed attributes and then to draw additional, tentative conclusions about these properties. Viaud's representation of a network of inferences generated by the observed properties, solid-head-at-right-angles-to-handle is illustrated in Figure 1.

Exercise

You are to examine the passage below and determine the identity of Country X, *a real country,* whose identity may be verified through analysis. You may use

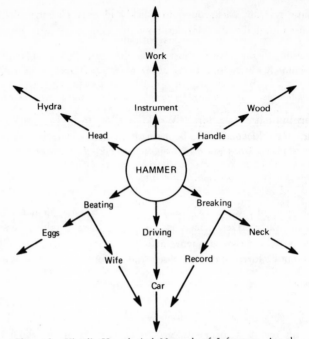

Figure 1. Viaud's Hypothetical Network of Inferences. An object or event is categorized as "hammer," and the process generates an inference network "hammer" having the rule "an instrument for beating, breaking, driving nails, etc., with a solid head at right angles to its handle." (Source: Gaston Viaud, *Intelligence: Its Evolution and Form*, E. J. Pomerans, trans., New York: Harper, 1960, p. 76.)

any strategy and consult any sources that you wish. Note the chain of events that take place in attempting to establish the identity of the country.

Country X differs from many other nations in several ways. It covers an area of 600,000 square miles with approximately 1,000,000 people. It is one huge plateau with the eastern half consisting mainly of plains sprinkled with mountains, while the western half is largely mountainous with some plains. Hundreds of lakes dot the country, particularly in the mountains, and clusters of forests are splashed throughout the hilly and mountainous regions.

Climatically, Country X suffers from cold winds that lash the treeless plains and from the harsh temperature extremes: for example, to 105° in the summer and to −50° in the winter.

Though fish are abundant, the people have not really cultivated a taste for them and exist chiefly on their livestock products and wild game.

Discussion

In using this exercise with groups that differ in terms of background, one may withhold or add salient facts. For example, the following passage provides more factual "clues" than the first and, as an alternate exercise, should allow one with little relevant background to quickly identify Country X. The added facts have been underlined. Consider how the additional facts provide salient clues.

Country X differs from many *of the* other *newly recognized* nations in several ways. It covers an area of 600,000 square miles (*population density less than two per square mile*). *Its people, largely nomadic, customarily dress in long flowing robes (dels) and live in canvas huts called yurts.*

Is is one huge plateau with the eastern half consisting mainly of plains sprinkled with mountains, while the western half is largely mountainous with some plains. *One-third of the country is covered by a desert but of this section only three percent is sandy; hence, the vast majority of the "desert" area can, in fact, support camels and some horses from its sparse vegetation.* Hundreds of lakes dot the country, particularly in the mountains, and clusters of forests are splashed throughout the hilly and mountainous regions.

Climatically, Country X suffers from cold winds that lash the treeless plains and from the harsh temperature extremes: for example, to 105° in the summer and to −50° in the winter.

Thus, neither the climate nor the geography is conducive to a strict agricultural way of life, and at the same time, the lack of abundant raw materials and suitable transportation lines inhibits industrial growth. The major occupation of the country, then, is herding; some small-scale industries—mainly to process livestock products—have been initiated.

Though fish are abundant *in the country's lakes,* the people have not really cultivated a taste for them and exist chiefly on their livestock products and wild game.

A LOGIC QUIZ

Whereas *inferences* suggest a likely conclusion, *implications* order a necessary conclusion. Black clouds *suggest* rain, but rain, in turn, *assures* wetness. The tragic joke of several decades ago, to the effect that the presence of Western Union delivery men in poverty neighborhoods represented tragedy, illustrates what occurs when the nuances between inference and implication are ignored. A basic element in accurate and sophisticated categorization, as well as logical analysis, is the ability to appreciate and identify this nuance.

The quiz, containing nine simple arguments, allows the reader to focus on a statement in a relatively straightforward, syllogistic form. In "real life," oral and written arguments seldom appear in this simplistic form; however, the intent of presenting the arguments in the manner of a basic quiz is to allow the reader to focus more clearly upon the structural relationship of the statement units.

Directions

Read over each of the following purported arguments and decide whether one who accepts its premises must *accept* its conclusion, that is, whether the conclusion is an *implication* of the premise. If your answer to this question is "yes," write "valid" on a separate answer sheet next to the number corresponding to the question. If your answer is "no," write "invalid."

Once you have completed the quiz, return to each question and analyze the categorical relationship among the items within each unit.

Quiz

1. Only a clever lawyer could have won an acquittal in this case. Mr. A. won an acquittal in this case. Mr. A. is therefore a clever lawyer.
2. This must be my cigarette; for all my cigarettes are on this table, and this cigarette is on this table.
3. All citizens are interested in political matters affecting the nation. All workers are citizens and therefore are interested in political matters affecting the nation.
4. All true humanitarians believe in the brotherhood of all men. All true Christians believe in the brotherhood of all men. Therefore, all true Christians are true humanitarians.
5. All machines are man-made. This automobile is man-made. It is therefore a machine.
6. Some communists are idealists. No idealists believe in the materialism of Karl Marx. Therefore, some communists do not believe in the materialism of Karl Marx.
7. All poisonous things are bitter. Potassium cyanide is not bitter. Therefore, potassium cyanide is not a poison.
8. All artists appeal to our emotions. All propagandists appeal to our emotions. All propagandists, therefore, are artists.
9. Most Americans speak of the United States as an Anglo-Saxon and Protestant country. Most Americans are neither Anglo-Saxon nor Protestant. Therefore, some persons who are neither Anglo-Saxon nor Protestant speak of the United States as an Anglo-Saxon and Protestant country.

Discussion

Answers to the quiz may be compared to those provided in the Appendix. Additionally, the categorical relationships among the statements are indicated by a series of circle diagrams.

It is recommended that those who feel they require more work in this area of logic consult a fundamental reference source,[1] since the operations required in the quiz are basic to a wide range of a social-studies teacher's classroom activities.

[1] For example, Robert H. Ennis, *Logic in Teaching* (Englewood Cliffs, N.J.: Prentice-Hall, 1969).

CONCEPT-IDENTIFICATION EXERCISE (CIE)

Unlike the preceding exercise, the CIE requires one to determine a class indentity, validate his choice by several methods, and then apply the concept to a new situation which the student must generate. In the exercise provided, a complex conjunctive concept is used. Complexity is measured here in terms of the number of criterial attributes (four) and the levels of abstraction characterizing the attributes.

The CIE has three parts, to be completed in the sequence indicated. It may be done by a small group, but it is best handled alone. A time limit of forty-five minutes is suggested, and the use of a Record Sheet, similar to the one in Figure 2, is recommended for the recording of responses.

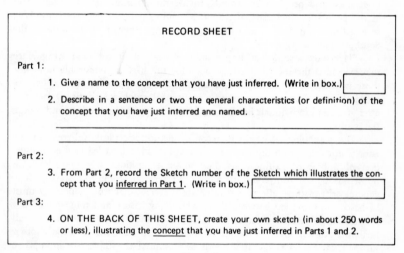

RECORD SHEET

Part 1:

    1. Give a name to the concept that you have just inferred. (Write in box.) ☐

    2. Describe in a sentence or two the general characteristics (or definition) of the concept that you have just inferred and named.

Part 2:

    3. From Part 2, record the Sketch number of the Sketch which illustrates the concept that you <u>inferred in Part 1</u>. (Write in box.) ☐

Part 3:

    4. ON THE BACK OF THIS SHEET, create your own sketch (in about 250 words or less), illustrating the <u>concept</u> that you have just inferred in Parts 1 and 2.

Figure 2

CIE—Part 1

Read the first *three* sketches carefully and supply the data requested on your Record Sheet under the heading "Part 1." Analyze the three sketches by focusign on the concept or class identity they all describe *in common,* even though they deal with different data.

    Sketch 1. The invention of the cotton gin by Eli Whitney in 1793 served to set in motion a chain of events. In the pre-cotton-gin era, wool and linen provided the primary substances for cloth-making in the Western World. Simplicity and efficiency of operation was the gin's forte, since it permitted the separation of cotton seeds from bolls at a far more rapid rate than could be achieved by hand alone. (Even the first crude gins were able to displace eight men per gin.) Furthermore, while the cotton gin at first needed hand power, it was later adapted to mechanical power. The time and effort saved by the gin, hence, led to cotton's maintaining a competitive edge over wool and linen as a desirable fiber for cloth-making. Subsequently, the lower price of cotton, in addition to its satisfactory cloth qualities, enabled it to rapidly replace woolen and linen cloth throughout the world.

In addition, since cotton plants were not congenial to most European soils (hot, humid climes and flat land areas were lacking), regions in Asia and Africa and the southern United States, for example, which did meet the necessary conditions, became potential cotton-growing centers. The American South, however, had an edge in that it already had convenient access to transportation routes, administrative talent, available markets, a ready labor supply, and eventually, centers for turning the cotton into fabric and clothing.

Areas of the South, like South Carolina, Georgia, Alabama, Mississippi, and Louisiana, rapidly became populated with potential cotton-growers, and a host of services grew up to meet their needs. There were people who would gin and transport the cotton; people who would sell farm, home and personal necessities; and people who would provide the entertainment facilities. And as the population increased, the South's waning political position since 1790 reversed its trend. Cotton and the gin, thus, strengthened the position of the Southern bloc in Congress.

Slaves now assumed an important economic role in cotton-growing, since they provided the source of cheap labor for the highly undesirable task—for those who could choose—of cotton-picking. Slave importation, hence, became common, even though such activity was illegal through constitutional mandate after 1809, and individuals became wealthy just by raising, trading, and selling slaves.

The psychological desire to reconcile democratic ideals inherent in the American culture with the idea of men owning other men led to the formulation of a host of justifications. Philosophical positions were put forth in numerous books, pamphlets, speeches, and sermons to justify slavery. The general drift of these efforts was to create the view that true democracy must be based on a division between those who enjoy leisure and those who labor so that others can have leisure. One strain of the argument tended to call forth the Ancient Greek example of a slave-based democracy; while another justified slavery on religious grounds and scoured the Bible for appropriate passages to buttress their position, while still another strain based its case on purported scientific findings which proved the racial superiority of whites over blacks and hence justified control of the slave.

Sketch 2. The net effect of the economic conditions which resulted in the "Great Depression" in 1929 was to cast considerable doubt on the value of old solutions to new problems. Great masses of people were economically depressed and existing institutions, both on the local and national level, simply did not function as effectively as they once had for the majority of the population. Pressing problems called for practical responses rather than a reliance on an "invisible hand."

President Hoover's response to the situation did not prove to be adequate, and the public's sensitivity to the need for new solutions was intensified. The series of actions and programs which evolved under the Franklin Roosevelt administration and which became known as the "New Deal" did provide the response that rose to the occasion and, in the process, introduced widespread social innovation. The most basic and far-reaching change it effected, as both its supporters and critics recognized, was a new perspective on the role of the federal government in resolving the problems of its citizens.

From this fundamental framework of change there flowed a series of specific institutional changes. Hence, millions of Americans steeped in orthodoxy about individual initiative (and input-output balancing in economic affairs) eventually could come to support or at least accept agricultural subsidies, unemployment insurance and social security in general, unbalanced budgets, major federal banking and currency reforms, federal subsidies to the arts, and federally sponsored utopian planning, as evidenced in the "Greenbelt" communities. Significantly, many of the revisions were and still are tolerated by those who were and are ignorant of their mechanics and rationale; deficit spending is an excellent example. What was grasped, however, was that the revisions provided some alleviation for the deeply felt problems; hence the intricacies of the cause-effect nexus were not so important.

In a similar vein, political institutions underwent major revisions in the New Deal period, as they were brought in line with new perspectives on the federal government. Correctly or incorrectly, the Democratic Party became identified as the symbol of concern with the needs of the common man and attracted, for years to come, the allegiance of the lower classes. Similarly, large blocs of Negro voters shifted their support from the party of Lincoln and remained Democrats until the Eisenhower era. Party bosses on the local level now lost much of the power that they had exercised by virtue of their ability to bestow favors on appreciative voters. Such "favors" in the New Deal period came to be accepted as the responsibility of the federal government toward its citizens.

Correspondingly, at lower levels of government political institutions were being reshaped to conform with the new, enlarged role of the federal government.

Sketch 3. (See Figures 3 and 4 and Table 1.)

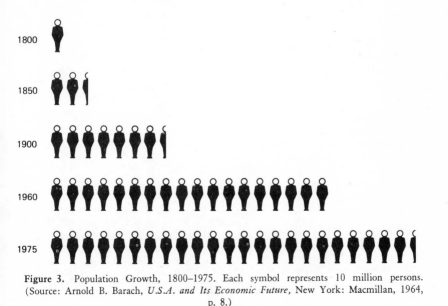

Figure 3. Population Growth, 1800–1975. Each symbol represents 10 million persons. (Source: Arnold B. Barach, *U.S.A. and Its Economic Future,* New York: Macmillan, 1964, p. 8.)

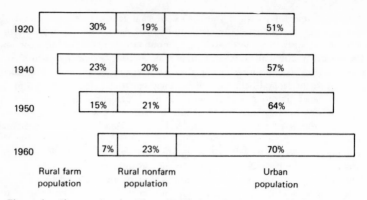

Figure 4. Changes in the Farm Population. (Source: Arnold B. Barach, *U.S.A. and Its Economic Future,* New York: Macmillan, 1964, p. 11.)

TABLE 1

POPULATION GROWTH OF THE UNITED STATES, 1790-1975

Year	Population Total in Thousands
1790	3,929
1800	5,308
1810	7,240
1820	9,638
1830	12,866
1840	17,069
1850	23,192
1860	31,443
1870	39,818
1880	50,156
1890	62,948
1900	75,995
1910	91,972
1920	105,711
1930	122,775
1940	131,669
1950	151,326
1960	179,323
1961	183,742
1962	186,591
1963	189,280
1970	214,200
1975	235,300

Source: Arnold B. Barach, *U.S.A. and Its Economic Future,* New York: Macmillan, 1964, p. 129.

CIE—Part 2

Each of the three *following* sketches illustrates a *different* concept. Select the sketch which illustrates the *same* concept that you inferred in Part 1. Record the *number* of this sketch on the Record Sheet under the heading Part 2.

Sketch 4. In the period following World War I the Ku Klux Klan was able to build its membership up to between four and five million by 1925. The Klan had moved to the North and had its greatest membership in Ohio and Indiana. Its program included the "Christian religion," "white supremacy," the protection of womenhood, "pure Americanism," states' rights, the destruction of lawlessness and foreign agitators, and the limitation of foreign immigration, among other points. It desired more and better patriotism, and set out to control church and state to achieve that end. It became involved with the contents of textbooks, entered political offices in many states, and took charge of public and private morals by floggings and displays of fiery crosses to bring "wrongdoers" back to the paths of virtue.

At its peak, it had elected many public officials, including governors, Senators, Congressmen, judges, and numerous local politicians. Police and sheriffs were frequently controlled by the Klan. Klansmen, themselves, were told not to believe what they read in the newspapers for it was said that the American press was controlled by Jews, Catholics, and immigrants. Many tradesmen, small businessmen, and generally middle-class Americans who belonged to the Klan came to believe that Negroes and foreigners constituted a real threat to American institutions.

Religion and the schools came in for careful attention by the Klan. It made numerous visitations to Protestant churches, leaving behind copies of the Bible or flags or even a money gift for the preacher. Decked out in hoods and sheets, the Klansmen found their church visitations to be good advertising for their organization. On the other hand, a parochial school was brought into conflict with the public school by the Klan. It called for a federal Department of Education with wide controls, Bible-reading in the schools, prominent display of the American flag, and the expulsion of non-American influences from the schools.

In each state the Klan had a central headquarters, but these did not have much control over the local klaverns. In the small, rural towns and in the decaying areas of urban, industrial neighborhoods, the local klaverns ruled themselves. They frequently made the decision to flog an errant soul or intimidate with a cross-burning. Often they arranged to drive through "Niggertown" with hoods and weapons, in order to remind the blacks to "stay in their place" or face the consequences. Occasionally, Klan members were even used by industrial leaders in the South to frighten off labor organizers.

The Ku Klux Klan was able to satisfy the craving of many Americans for excitement and to provide the outlet for their pet hatreds. For thousands, its pagentry of robes and burning crosses and its acts of violence gave a sense of dignity and importance, although false, and a measure of control over those they hated and feared.

Sketch 5. In 1954 when Congress was concerned about the amassing of approximately $4 billion worth of surplus farm commodities in connection with the agricultural price-support program, it enacted the Agricultural Trade Development Act (known as P. L. 480). Under the law over $9 billion worth of farm products were disposed of abroad within an eight-year period. Some items were bartered or donated, but most of them were shipped to underdeveloped countries to be paid for in their own currency—an extremely important and valuable concession to nations who were short on our dollars. The United States, in turn, has used a portion of counterpart funds to make loans to these countries and to finance its expenses in them, such as research, educational-exchange and technical-assistance expenditures. The funds have been used also to develop and expand agricultural markets for United States farmers. The program, in general, has had numerous foreign and domestic benefits, and the cooperation of both sides has been an important factor in the success of the program.

The production and distribution of a specific agricultural product often involves a similar international relationship. The Sugar Act of several years' vintage had authorized the Department of Agriculture to determine annual sugar requirements of consumers in the United States and to establish marketing or import quotas for the various sugar-producing areas, here and abroad, which supplied this market. The program was set up when the sugar industry was suffering and so was designed to promote the interests of American producers and of those sugar-producing nations which were friendly to the United States, while providing American consumers with an assured sugar supply at reasonable prices.

But in the early 1960's, this system of market control was disturbed when Castro's regime provoked the United States into an embargo of Cuban goods, including sugar. At that point, the Department of Agriculture decided to compensate for the lost Cuban sugar supply by decreeing higher production and import quotas for other production areas, both foreign and domestic. By 1964, however, domestic sugar yields had increased to the point where additional acreage allotments for sugar beet production were being turned down. This fact then complicated the question of whether to renew sugar import quotas. Not to do so would obviously distress foreign producers who had geared their productions to the demands we once established; to *do* so, however, would be to jeopardize the profits of U. S. producers.

Sketch 6. Those Americans who, because of the color of their skin or certain physical characteristics, had been denied rights granted to other citizens, began to make their maximum efforts against segregation policies in the mid-1950's. A minority of this group of Americans joined into groups like the Black Muslims, who espoused apartheid and black supremacy. Other Negro groups, dissatisfied with the status quo—but with different goals—rebelled against older, established groups working to combat discrimination, such as the National Association for the Advancement of Colored People. These sorts of groups were challenged as not effecting equality rapidly enough.

Thus organizations which were more militant and activist sprang up. Through groups like the Congress of Racial Equality (CORE), young blacks pressed for equality through what became known as "sit-ins," demanding the right to eat at lunch counters or in restaurants, to use books at libraries in common with whites, or to share bus and theatre seats with their white brethren. Furthermore, Negroes and whites conducted "freedom rides" together, often attended by violent opposition on the part of segregationists, in order to desegregate interstate busses and terminals. Many of them, too, were arrested in mass demonstrations and subsequently jailed. Demonstrations then spread to the North, with mass attacks against *de facto* and deliberate segregation in housing, employment practices, and schools. And in the summer of 1963, over 200,000 black and white demonstrators—many of them religious leaders of all faiths—bodily delivered their concern over segregation to Congress in a "march on Washington."

Through the Attorney General's office, the Kennedy administration lent its power to the civil rights struggle: Pressure was applied to achieve the integration of interstate transportation; the right of a Negro to attend the all-white University of Mississippi was supported with armed might; and a comprehensive civil-rights bill designed to achieve equal rights for all Americans was drawn up and forwarded to Congress. Later, under President Johnson, such a bill was passed as the impetus of the movement gained support from the majority of Americans. The mass media, especially television, played a key role in forming such support by bringing to the attention of the nation the many atrocities committed against civil-rights demonstrators.

In the aftermath of the struggle and the passage of the Act, the integration of schools—in the North and in the South—began to proceed at a more rapid rate. Furthermore, the movement had served to unite religious leaders of all faiths in a common effort and generally worked to commit the more conservative religions to a greater involvement in needed secular reforms.

The principle of "nonviolence" was now an accepted effective method of combating injustice and introduced a relatively new political weapon into the American social fabric. Negroes, too, seemed on the way to uniting their numbers into a political and economic bloc in the nation at large and especially in the South. The upshot of such unification in the South was the beginnings of a realignment of political and economic mores in communities and states affected. Merchants who discriminated in hiring employees, for example, were confronted with black boycotts which spelled the difference between profit and loss; similarly, candidates for public office at the local level now had to appeal to a bloc of voters which contained a minority of whites; adjustments in political appeals and promises reflected this shift.

CIE—Part 3

On the *back* of your Record Sheet, create your *own* sketch (in about 250 words or less) illustrating the concept that you have *just inferred* in Parts 1 and 2.

Make your sketch as specific as you can within the space limitations given. Use *any* data you wish and do *not* be concerned if some of your data is inaccurate. You are to focus on illustrating *just the concept that you have inferred in Parts 1 and 2*. By developing your own sketch with different data, you are demonstrating that you can apply the concept.

Discussion

By consulting the Appendix, one may compare his responses in Parts 1 and 2 with those used to establish the design of the CIE. The Part 3 response may be compared to some representative sketches recorded by those who have completed the CIE. Previous use of the CIE with teachers seem to indicate that prior instruction in the nature of concept learning significantly improves one's performance, and that individuals fare better working alone than in groups.

The use of figures and tables in Sketch 3 indicates also how relevant facts may be organized in a variety of formats (pictures, films, recordings, drawings, etc.) in addition to conventional text narrative.

AN APPLICATION EXERCISE

In this exercise one is required to apply the constructs discussed in earlier passages and the general principles and structure employed in the preceeding exercise. The reader is asked to develop a prototype of a CIE that might be appropriate for a given age level of children, keeping in mind the characteristics of a selected group of social-science concepts and the learning styles of the students in question.

Assignment

1. Indicate the age level of the population for which you plan to develop a CIE.
2. Select a concept from the list of social-science concepts in the Appendix appropriate to the population identified.
3. Develop a CIE by organizing sketches with both a format and facts appropriate to the population identified.
4. Develop a Record Sheet with a format appropriate to the population identified.
5. Administer the CIE and evaluate the results.

Discussion

The development of a CIE for kindergarten and first-grade youngsters (and perhaps older) will probably involve the construction of sketches that use only nonreading and three-dimensional, manipulable material (objects); the same is true for the format of the Record Sheet, which in part may take the form of, for example, verbal responses or "projects."

Another consideration in this assignment is that when the issue of appropriateness is in doubt, the CIE may function as a possible test. If a youngster performs well by the criteria established in advance of administering the CIE, then the concept and sketches may be considered appropriate for him.

AN EXPERIMENTAL RESEARCH PROJECT

The final exercise takes the form of an experimental research study to measure the extent to which a given population of students has mastered a given concept. *Experimental research* is that which applies a true experimental research design to a setting in which carefully prescribed and manipulated conditions are operative.[2] Its value is that it affords a teacher some reasonably well-regulated measures of the effect of an instructional sequence. With this approach, a teacher need not interrupt her usual teaching procedures to any great extent, and she is better able to make supportable generalizations concerning the impact of her teaching procedures under usual operating conditions.

While experimental research is not a common thing among classroom teachers, the project recommended herein should be within the capabilities of neophyte researchers.[3] Its design is basic but rigorous, and only fundamental statistical procedures are required to generate the conclusions.

Design and Procedures

This design is referred to as "The Post-test Only Control Group Design."[4] It involves assigning one's total population of students (N) to two groups by randomized selection procedures. This process provides the greatest assurance that the two groups initially are basically equal in their potential ability to learn a given concept. The group designated as the experimental group may then be assigned the treatment (concept learning instruction), while the remainder of the population (control group) receives alternate or no instruction. Both groups are measured for their level of concept mastery by some criterion measures immediately upon completion of the experiment.

The degree of difference between the measures may be evaluated by a simple t test[5] to determine if the experimental group has performed significantly better than the control group. One's hypothesis is that there *will* indeed be a significant difference in favor of the population receiving the favored instruction, and by recasting this assumption in the form of the null hypothesis, "There will be no significant difference between the two groups with respect to scores on a concept-mastery test," one is able to reject or accept the notion through basic statistical means.

---

[2] See the discussion in Donald T. Campbell and Julian C. Stanley, "Experimental and Quasi-Experimental Designs for Research on Teaching," *Handbook of Research on Teaching*, N. L. Gage, ed. (Chicago: Rand McNally, 1963), pp. 171–246.

[3] For additional assistance, consult a basic educational research text, such as Gilbert Sax, *Empirical Foundations of Educational Research* (Englewood Cliffs, N.J.: Prentice-Hall, 1968).

[4] Campbell and Stanley, *op. cit.*, p. 195.

[5] *Ibid.*, p. 196.

Discussion

While this project is limited in its scope, it provides at least a basic index of the degree of success a teacher is having in concept teaching. It also suggests a means by which a teacher may compare various strategies for teaching concepts, since the instructional treatment may take any form or format that the teacher wishes. Similarly, a criterion measure of mastery might take a variety of forms, either those suggested in the Appendix or ones of the teacher's making.

One may regard an individual class or a series of classes as his total population. An elementary teacher might wish to make her self-contained class the N, whereas a secondary teacher might use his entire five classes in the total population.

One of the more critical considerations in this exercise is that of time. The sooner that the instructional process can be completed after its initiation and the sooner that the criterion measure can be administered after the completion of instruction, the less likely is the experiment to be invalidated by extraneous variables.

CONCLUSION

All of the foregoing exercises, with some modifications, may be used with a wide range of age levels among elementary and secondary youngsters, as well as adult populations. In general, they provide some actual, cognitive involvement with different dimensions of the concept-learning process. Moreover, they should suggest some instructional considerations for assisting others in mastering concepts and acquiring necessary prerequisite skills. To the extent that one has followed the drift of the discussion in the preceding chapters, the exercises should also allow one to relate and incorporate his insights into classroom-related activities.

SUGGESTED READINGS

Ennis, Robert H. *Logic in Teaching*. Englewood Cliffs, N.J.: Prentice-Hall, 1969.

An in-depth examination of fundamental principles of logic designed for teachers. This book is of particular value to those who have had little or no formal training in logic.

Sax, Gilbert, *Empirical Foundations of Educational Research*. Englewood Cliffs, N.J.: Prentice-Hall, 1968.

A lucid, cogent, well-written text outlining principles and practices of educational research in a form that is easily applied by teachers.

CHAPTER 9

Concept Learning in the Social-Studies Curriculum: Some Directions for the Future

Without question, the current spate of social-studies curricula emanating from university-based projects, from commercial publishers, and from school-based teacher committees across the United States reflect a consistent verbal commitment to a concept-oriented approach. To the extent that shibboleths can be regarded as substitutes for substance, curricula designed for effecting concept learning dominate the current elementary and secondary social-studies field.

Equally without question, the current literature reflects a better conceptual grasp of and empirical basis for the nature of concept learning. While schema differ and experimental research conclusions vary in some respects, there appears to be a greater consensus today among social-studies curriculum shapers concerning the basic characteristics of a concept and its relative importance in the range of cognitive studies than ever before. A variety of factors may explain how relative agreement on this point has evolved.

1. The increasing emphasis in the past decade on the *cognitive* domain of intellectual activities has channeled more comparative data into the field.
2. Greater concern in educational research for specification of microvariables and quantification in general has moved the attention from more global processes like "thinking," "categorizing," and "generalizing."
3. Curriculum builders have become more sensitive toward and knowledgable about psychological processes in general.
4. More serious and systematic attention has been devoted to analyzing the verbal discourse of youngsters within and without classrooms.
5. The influence of Jerome Bruners's work upon curriculum developers.
6. The increasing infusion of the behavioral-science disciplines into the curricular scene has further underscored the classic query, "What knowledge is of most worth?" and subsequently made more urgent the issue of *how* to determine such answers.

In the face of rhetorical emphasis upon concepts in the social-studies curriculum, the lack of disagreement concerning the nature and importance of concepts among social-studies educators, and the presence of increasing literature concerning concepts, certain expectations about the social-studies curriculum appear in order. At least three general expectations seem in order: (1) a given concept or set of concepts that are specified in operational terms will provide the basis for some dimension of a social-studies curricular sequence; (2) the operational specifications for the concept(s) will be used to assemble only relevant subject matter to facilitate a learning situation; and (3) students who interact with the assembled curriculum will have learned the given concepts as a result of their interaction with it.

There is a serious question about whether these expectations are realized in most of the social-studies curricula that indicate a desire to emphasize the learning of concepts.

SOME SPECIFICATIONS FOR CURRICULA

Organizations of Materials

Materials explicitly tailored to the selected models of concept learning that we have discussed in earlier chapters (or any other models) would, of course, vary considerably in their details. Generically, however, materials that purport to aid in the learning of explicit concepts would share these fundamental, common properties.

1. The concept(s) to be learned from the materials would be operationally delineated in the teacher's instructions.
2. They would contain explicit exemplars and nonexemplars of the concept(s) in question and be identified as such in a variety of subject-matter contexts.
3. Insofar as possible, extraneous material (i.e., that which is neither used as an exemplar nor a nonexemplar) would be omitted or, through structuring and focusing, identified explicitly as extraneous.

The character of most of the materials, broadly construed, that are currently available would be altered seriously if these implications were translated into practice. For one thing, the traditional concern for narrative continuity, common to history materials, for example, appears to be a significant variable only insofar as it may be a source of extraneous data. So-called "enrichment" materials may function in a similar way.

A word here concerning so-called "behavioral objectives" and the current emphasis being placed upon their specification seems pertinent. Seen as a *means* rather than an end, concern with the specification of objectives in terms of observable student behavior may help to focus needed attention upon the analysis of an appropriate instructional procedure, discriminating relevant from irrelevant details. Clearly, however, behavioral objectives, of themselves, do *not* imply corresponding instructional procedures, and consequently do not provide adequate guidance for the structuring of subject matter. To state an objective behaviorally concerning a concept-learning task, then, is *not* to state the design of a learning process. Presumably, however, one who follows some model of concept learning (either those discussed in preceding chapters or others) could supply on demand behaviorally oriented statements of his objectives. What is at issue in this analysis is the matter of perspective concerning the role of behavioral objectives in developing curricula for facilitating concept learning. While they may serve as analytical tools, the reader is cautioned to observe the maxim, "Never let a behavioral objective interfere with your objective." He is also cautioned to heed David Ausubel's conclusion: "It is probably more realistic and generally satisfactory to define educational objectives in grosser or more descriptive terms that are closer to the language of the curriculum worker than to that of the psychologist."[1]

Books and Texts. If organized to promote concept learning, textual materials might be organized around concept units containing sequenced exemplars and nonexemplars from a variety of different contexts. Focusing instructions, questions, and practice opportunities would be provided within the unit. Exemplars and nonexemplars might consist of case studies or sketches, pictures, graphs, tables and charts, or drawings. These might be arranged in a variety of patterns—in chronological order, in a general topical or theoretical frame of reference, according to a particular social-science discipline, or in order of ascending complexity.

Films and Videotapes. Films and videotapes represent an excellent vehicle for regulating, through visual cues and oral prompts, one's focus upon exemplars and nonexemplars. Constructed for concept learning, they would *exclude,* insofar as possible, all irrelevant materials and would omit the story-drama structure that social-studies films have traditionally used. A parenthetical note here is appropriate concerning the much heralded eight-mm. "single-concept" loop films. While so proclaimed, the social-studies eight-mm. loops currently available *are not* in general designed to meet the three general criteria cited for the organization of materials. What they *do* provide (and many reasonably well) is a short (three- to five-minute) film clip of a particular historical event, usually through reprints of primary-source film or recreated events and normally without sound or focusing instructions other than descriptive comments.

The author *has* located two films which, while *not* designed for this purpose nor advertised as such, fit the general specifications cited for materials: *Neighbours,* a nine-minute film by Norman McLaren, using human animation and dealing with "conflict;" and "*Model Man,*" a seventeen-minute film produced by the Econ 12 social studies project dealing with "models."

Slides, Drawings, and Pictures. At the expense perhaps of some visual impact, slides, drawings, and pictures afford an added opportunity to edit and shape more carefully than films, exemplars, and nonexemplars. When synchronized with

---

[1] David P. Ausubel, *Educational Psychology: A Cognitive View* (New York: Holt, 1968), p. 35.

a dialogue focus and instructions, they allow for considerable control over the characteristics of the material *actually* presented to the learner. DeCecco has drawn the interesting conclusion, for example, that "direct experience or realistic examples are usually not preferable to simplified presentations of the concepts, such as line drawings, cartoons, diagrams, and charts."[2]

Audiotapes. Audiotapes may be seen as functioning in essentially the same way as strictly textual material, providing only an auditory substitute for the written page. While the advent of cassettes provides a technologically efficient way to harness audio material, the chief values of tape would seem to be for *non-readers* and for use in conjunction with other media forms.

Field Trips. Field trips, perceived in a special perspective, can provide powerful concrete exemplars and nonexemplars. A high-school class studying about "central business districts," for example, has an easy opportunity to use field trips for purposes of examining concrete exemplars and nonexemplars, if appropriate focusing instructions and questions are provided. Field trips, then, when seen as opportunities for single-focus examination of examples and non-examples of concepts rather than global cognitive assaults on "interesting places," provide one of the few *concrete* sources of materials open to social-studies teachers.

Combined Media. The "combined" refers simply to situations in which media are used in a *complementary* way. Usually, this will be done for purposes of variety (e.g. texts, then pictures, then charts, etc.), to supplement the limitations of one form of media (e.g. adding needed pictoral features to text, providing aural instructions with slides or still pictures, etc.), or to compensate for student limitations, (e.g. inability to read, a physical handicap such as deafness, etc.).

Certainly it would be inappropriate and pointless for *all* curricular materials to be designed along the lines indicated in the foregoing discussion, and no such suggestion is intended. Rather, the intent is to suggest that if one's objective is to teach *concepts* instead of, for example, specifically relating descriptive information, developing fact-connections, examining values, teaching motor skills, or even teaching generalizations, the curricular materials he uses should be so structured as to maximize a student's likelihood of learning the concept. That not all these competing goals are mutually exclusive and incompatible with the simultaneous goal of concept learning is perhaps true. But curricular development has not begun to even approach the stage where materials are constructed in this complex fashion to achieve multiple goals; moreover, it is difficult to analyze logically what the theoretical structure of such materials might be.

Organization of Instructional Sequences

All of the traditional unresolved questions and issues relating to the articulation of generically similar and dissimilar instructional objectives apply to the

---

[2] John P. DeCecco, *The Psychology of Learning and Instruction* (Englewood Cliffs, N.J.: Prentice-Hall, 1968), p. 412.

teaching of concepts. In other words, what is the sequential relationship of concept teaching to other instructional processes dealing with the social studies? "Other processes" include teaching generalizations, teaching motor skills, providing perceptual experiences, allowing opportunities for aesthetic development and humanistic considerations, teaching valuing, and developing skill in questioning, research, inference-generation, logical analysis, and sensitivity for the concerns of others. The sequential and emphasis priority of these instructional processes needs to be established, at least as working hypotheses, for inter- and intragrade levels generally.

Moreover, there are important considerations concerning the relationship of coordinate, subordinate, and supraordinate concepts that are nested within the preceding issues. Hence, there is a need to examine not only the sequential relationship between all types of instructional sequences but also the interrelationship of instructional sequences designed explicitly for teaching concepts.

Characteristics of Instructional Sequences

Instructional sequences designed to produce the learning of given concepts may be characterized by a variety of maneuvers, as the models discussed in the preceding chapters indicated. Two general characteristics, however, appear in all the models—the presence of conscious design and a theory of instruction.

The Presence of Conscious Design. Any instructional sequence reflects an overall objective, either defensible or indefensible. Not infrequently beginning teachers, on particularly traumatic days, have as their general objective (often explicitly stated and almost always defensible) "to get through this day (week)!" Stating one's overall objective for teaching social studies not only opens one's approach to rational scrutiny but also allows for self-determination of what shall be given *priority* in social-studies classes, where an excess of "worthwhile" subject matter always exists.

In concert with clear specification of objectives, a knowledge base about instruction in general is reflected. Included in this knowledge base are instructional models, related research on instruction, key variables that affect instruction, analysis of instructional failures, and most importantly, perhaps, direct experience with cause-effect relationships in real or simulated instructional settings, in which one can analyze learning outcomes as a function of instructional sequences.

The notion of conscious design also includes a logical analysis of the learning tasks that have been planned, including the contingencies predicated and the hypothetical feedback anticipated. This step does not preclude instructional sequences that are "open-ended" or that have unpredictable outcomes; rather, it prepares the teacher for a variety of possibilities as an instructional sequence unfolds.

Theory of Instruction. It may be recalled that in a preceding chapter a theory was regarded as an invention under which related concept—and interrelated fact—clusters are subsumed in a special logical structure. A theory of instruction, then, may be viewed as a network of logically related notions about how, why, and under what circumstances instruction should occur, the diverse properties of instruction, and the ways in which its impact may be detected. In relationship to teachers and students, a theory of instruction would include specifically, for example, such information as: (a) generalizations concerning a teacher's and students' assumed roles; (b) knowledge of methodological alternatives; (c) knowledge of teaching strategies and their appropriate placement; (d) a repertoire of instructional techniques; and (e) procedures for evaluating instruction.

A possible model for a theory of instruction encompassing the foregoing points in relationship to effecting concept learning is provided in Figure 1. *Method,* similar to the definition applied by Hunt and Metcalf,[3] is assumed to

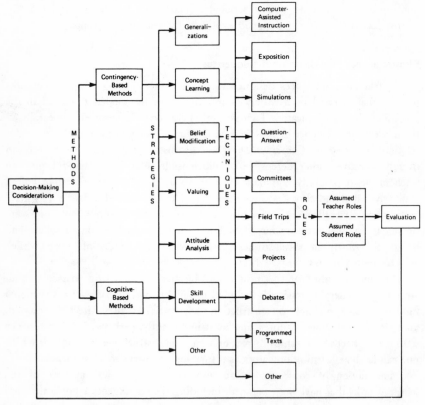

Figure 1.   Model of a Theory of Instruction.

[3] Maurice P. Hunt and Lawrence E. Metcalf, *Teaching High School Social Studies: Problems in Reflective Thinking and Social Understanding,* 2d ed. (New York: Harper, 1968), p. 171.

be one's perspective concerning what psychological conditions allow the most significant learning to take place and concerning what the goals and functions of education should be. *Strategy* is defined as the specific way in which a method is applied to a particular instructional task or set of tasks. The structural relationship of facts then defines the individual identity of a strategy, and consistent with a given methodology, one may opt for a variety of compatible strategies for instruction. *Technique*, again using Hunt and Metcalf's definition, refers to the format or communication vehicle used to convey a strategy; lectures, films and other visual media, computer-assisted instruction, simulations, and the like may all be viewed as techniques.[4]

Also illustrated in Figure 1 is the *order* of operations, from left to right, that a teacher would follow in applying some components of a theory of instruction, once entry behaviors have been ascertained. Thus method options are prior to strategy options, which are prior to technique selection, which precedes the definition of role relationships, and evaluation provides a feedback mechanism for the theory.

Individualizing Concept Learning: Curricular Considerations for Students and Teachers

Operating within the context of a concept-oriented approach to curricula, flexibility is provided for the selection of alternative subject-matter areas and varying degrees of analysis and study. From the perspective of a student, freedom is provided for selecting subject-matter exemplars that match with some interest areas and for pursuing a topic to any depth he wishes beyond the basic criterion measures for the concept-learning task. Harking back to an earlier illustration, a student who expressed some interests, for example, concerning congressional activities, "big business" in the early twentieth century, and racial issues, might have his exemplars selected from these general topical areas for purposes of learning a concept of "power."

Similarly, a teacher has some measure of freedom in selecting exemplars from areas in which his competencies and interests are greatest. A teacher, for example, with a high degree of competency in facets of European history and with a general interest in institutional processes could draw upon these contexts in framing his exemplars. To the extent that such student-profile-subject-matter-teacher-profile matches are possible, concept-oriented curricula provide a dual measure of individualization not possible in programs where specific textual material is itself an end. In the latter approach, teacher and student learning goals are shaped almost exclusively and narrowly by their curricula. Individualization therein, to the extent that it exists at all, is a function only of learning rate and teaching style.

[4] *Ibid.*, pp. 171 and 175–184.

AREAS FOR RESEARCH

While concept learning as an objective is currently receiving considerable emphasis in the social-studies literature and in the descriptive literature accompanying curricular materials, little evidence has been experimentally adduced concerning how students systematically learn *social-science* concepts. A variety of categories of researchable problems exist that might provide more empirical evidence for transfer to *social-studies* classrooms. For example, two questions currently under investigation by the author are:

1. What are the effects of varying degrees of extraneous material upon the learning of less complex conjunctive social science concepts?
2. What are the effects of varying ratios of positive and negative exemplars upon the learning of less complex conjunctive concepts?

Other issues that might be investigated include:

3. In what ways do the learning of disjunctive and relational social-science concepts differ from the learning of conjunctive concepts?
4. What are the effects of different types of materials and media upon the learning of social-science concepts?
5. What are the effects of instructional set or cueing upon a concept-learning task?
6. What are the effects of training in categorizing and drawing inferences upon the learning of social-science concepts?
7. Developmentally, what differences in the learning of social-science concepts can be specified for subjects of varying ages?
8. What is the optimal learning pattern for subordinate, coordinate, and supraordinate social-science concepts?
9. What concept-learning hierarchies can be ascertained for social-science concepts?
10. What are the various affective components of concept learning?

A particularly fruitful area of exploration relates to the effects of printed instructional material upon the learning of social science-concepts, about which little is known. "Validation of such effects," Frayer and Klausmeier note, "would have important implications for textbook writing."[5] They suggest a research paradigm which incorporates may of the issues listed above.[6]

---

[5] Dorothy A. Frayer and Herbert J. Klausmeier, "Effects of Instructional Variations on Mastery of Geometric Concepts by Fourth- and Sixth-Grade Children," Paper presented at the annual meeting of the *American Educational Research Association,* March 2–6, 1970, Minneapolis, Minnesota, p. 1.

[6] *Ibid.*

Research dealing with learning of subject matter concepts requires extension of the techniques used in laboratory studies. First, concepts must be analyzed to determine their relevant and irrelevant characteristics. This analysis provides a rational basis for teaching the concept and testing for understanding. Second, variables manipulable in printed instructional material must be identified. These variables may include some not usually considered in laboratory studies, such as use of definitions, synonyms, and sentence contexts. Third, various aspects of concept learning should be tested. These tests should go beyond simple recognition of examples and nonexamples, to determine knowledge of relevant characteristics, definition, and relationships to other concepts. Finally, studies should be carried out with subjects of various ages to discover possible interactions between age and instructional variables.

ANALYZING THE CURRICULUM-REFORM PROCESS[7]

All those who wish to reform some area of the curriculum require some sensitivity for the dynamics of the reform process—specifically, for how changes in one component of a school system affect and are affected by other components within the system. In short, even if one's concern is to reform only the social-studies curriculum within a school by introducing new materials designed to facilitate concept learning, his analysis of change processes must go well beyond the parameters of his narrow focus to include the entire school system.

Perhaps surprisingly, in view of the numerous historical precedents from which to draw, curricular reform at the local level has often been ineffective and short-lived. Not infrequently, reform, however explicitly or implicitly defined, has been hastily planned, limited in the scope of its effects to a few members of the total school system, and sensitive to only a few variables within the system. The net effect of these shortcomings usually is failure to disseminate and diffuse reform throughout a school system.

It is the dimension of task analysis of the dynamics of curricular reform to which the reader is now directed. Presumably, by perceiving a school complex or district as a "system" with attendant "subsystems," one may better teach and interrelate a greater number of key variables involved in any reform process.

A systems-orientation, Rosove states,[8] "attempts to view a problem in terms of multiple, rather than single, variables, or factors. It attempts to isolate and solve a problem as a total entity, rather than as a series of unrelated elements." Such an approach requires one to conceptualize curricular reform in a wide perspective, while still focusing on solving smaller problems.

[7] This discussion, with minor modifications, is taken from Peter H. Martorella, "Curricular Change: A Paradigm for Analyzing the Parameters of Curricular Reform," *Educational Technology,* in press.

[8] Perry E. Rosove, *An Analysis of Possible Future Roles of Educators As Derived from a Contextual Map.* SP-3088 (Santa Monica, Calif.: System Development Corporation, March 8, 1968), p. 28.

A Systems Model

In a recent paper[9] W. W. Herrmann presented a hypothetical model representing the operative relationships between government agencies, constraints and objectives that is useful for conceptualizing the dynamics of curricular reform. While the structural form of his paradigm is fundamental, its analytical import is powerful. In essence, it requires a reformer to analyze his task in terms of correlating his objectives with the resource strengths and deficiencies within the system, permits him to specify more accurately his resource needs from outside the system, and allows him to follow more clearly the patterns of reform through subsets.

If one represents all the personnel and items which, when taken together, comprise a school or school district by the area within a rectangle, as in Figure 2,

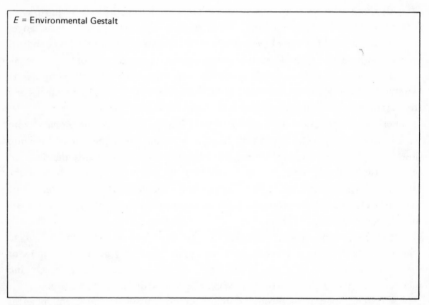

Figure 2. Environmental Gestalt. The set of all things—tangible and intangible, animate and inanimate—common to a given school system or consortium of school systems.

it may be referred to as the *Environmental Gestalt of the School System.* This latter phrase may be seen as applying to the set of all elements—tangible and intangible, animate and inanimate—common to a given school system or consortium of school systems.

Within the environmental gestalt of the total school system, the curriculum

---

[9] William W. Hermann, *Public Order in a Free Society: A Problem in Suboptimization,* SP-2989 (Santa Monica, Calif.: System Development Corporation, April 8, 1968).

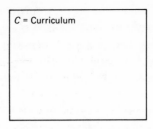

Figure 3. The set of all elements comprising the curriculum that are operative in a given school system.

may be perceived as a subset, as shown in Figure 3. However a particular person may choose to define the school's curriculum, it exists as a component or set within the total school complex.

The relationship between the set of items defined as the curriculum and the school complex may be represented as in Figure 4.

A common concern of many involved in curricular reform relating to concept learning is the category of behaviors known as "teaching strategies" or pedagogical moves, which are designed to produce certain learning outcomes. This class of maneuvers may be seen as a subset of curriculum and diagrammed as a circle

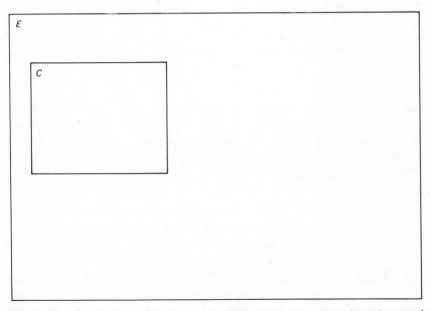

Figure 4. The set of all elements comprising the curriculum that are within the environmental gestalt of a given school system.

within the smaller box, as indicated in Figure 5. Any other subset upon which one prefers to focus may be substituted for the analysis.

To illustrate one further level, Figure 6 represents one category, curricular materials, within the subset C_T. Curricular materials may be viewed here as one component of a teaching strategy, designated as C_{TM}. The implications of Figure

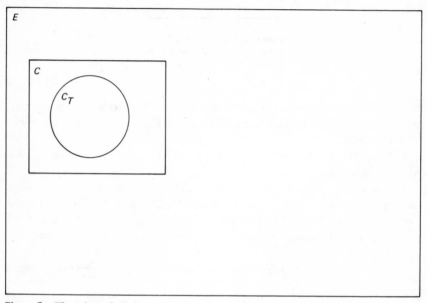

Figure 5. The subset of all elements of the curriculum related to teaching strategies C_T, within the curriculum C, that is within a given environmental gestalt E.

6 are that all curricular materials within the context of curriculum are part of teaching strategies. Those who find this definitional relationship uncomfortable might prefer to substitute "learning strategies" for "teaching strategies," which will inject a different emphasis into the analysis. In order to isolate that dimension of the system which one wishes to reform, it is possible to manipulate both categories and degrees of subsystems in developing an analysis of the system.

Curricular Objectives

Obviously, all components of the system have some objectives, and the relationship between each can also be illustrated. In general, the characteristics of objectives parallel those of their related components. Thus, for the set of all activities classified as the curriculum C, there exist a set of objectives O^C; for the subset teaching strategies C_T, there are corresponding objectives O^C_T; and for that element of the subset C_T that was classified as subject matter C_{TM}, there is a category of objectives O^C_{TM}. This relationship between components and objectives is presented in Figure 7.

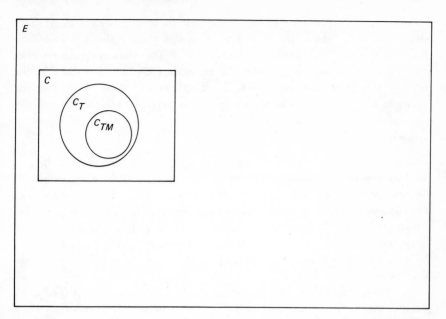

Figure 6. The element of curricular materials C_{TM} as a component of the subset of all elements of the curriculum related to teaching strategies C_T that are but one portion of the set of elements comprising the total curriculum C, within a given environment E.

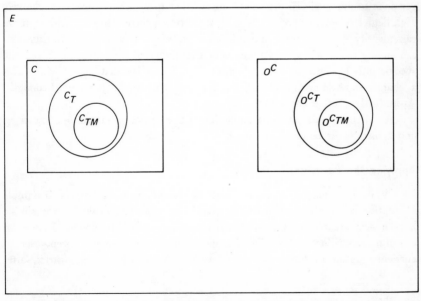

Figure 7. Curriculum, teaching strategies, and curricular materials and corresponding objectives in terms of sets, subsets, and elements within a given environment.

What any curriculum reformer would now do well to heed is Herrmann's observation that, "one of the obvious issues at this point is the degree of compatibility between the different sets of objectives."[10] The relationship, for example, between the objectives of the curricular materials (represented perhaps by the implicit or explicit objective of a textbook writer) and those of the teaching strategies is a crucial nexus frequently ignored in curricular-reform attempts.

Constraints

Any school system includes a set of constraints which interact with the curriculum and its objectives. Their interaction may be truly characterized as dynamic because constraints may interact with the shaping of the objectives and the curriculum and vice versa. The same arbitrary principles of categorization which applied to the curriculum and its subsets and their elements hold for constraints. What is more important here than categories for purposes of curricular reform is the exhaustive listing of all possible operative constraints within the system.

For purposes of illustration, constraints will be classified as Legal, Technical, Administrative, Attitudinal, Economic, Commitments, and Expertise, since these seem to be fairly exhaustive. This aggregate of constraints may be regarded as a set, indicated by a rectangle, and each individual constraint is a circle within the new rectangle. This new set is then related to the total system, as shown in Figure 8.

In observing the relationship among constraints, Herrmann's caution again is germane to our analysis: "It would appear that there actually exists a relatively high degree of interaction and dependency between these elements. Although we can identify the maximum and minimum *number* of possible interactions, we cannot say too much at this time about the *nature* of the interactions and the specific interdependencies."[11] At best, one could only speculate about what effect a change in Administrative policies, for example, might have on Economic, Attitudinal, or other constraints.

An attempt to depict the dynamic interaction between curriculum, objectives, and constraints is reflected in Figure 9.

Applying the Paradigm

While the analysis of each system is unique in some respect, a sample illustration contrasting a nonparadigm and the paradigm at work in a simple hypothetical situation may be useful. Let us assume that Mr. Eager, Curriculum Coordinator of Zilch School District, wishes to introduce new concept-oriented curricular materials into every social-studies course within the district, after

[10] *Ibid.*, p. 14.
[11] *Ibid.*, pp. 17–18.

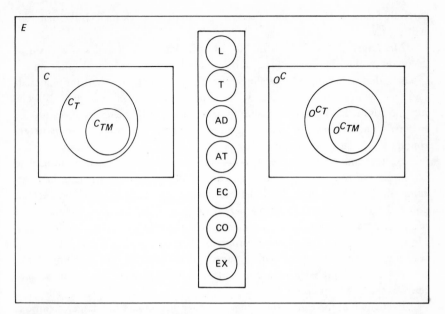

Figure 8. Elements of curriculum, objectives of the curriculum, and constraints as sets within a given environment, where L = Legal Constraints; T = Technical Constraints; AD = Administrative Constraints; AT = Attitudinal Constraints; EC = Economic Constraints; CO = Commitment Constraints; EX = Expertise Constraints.

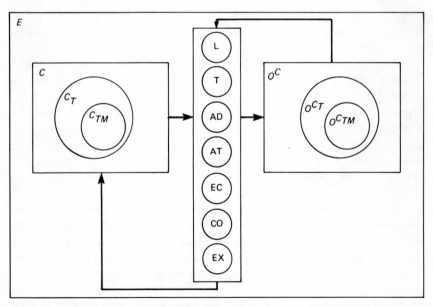

Figure 9. A hypothetical model representing the operative relationships between curriculum, constraints, and objectives.

carefully formulating some concept-learning objectives which he feels the materials will satisfy.

Mr. Eager works through the norms operative in Zilch and sets a chain of events in motion. He pleads his case before the board for additional funds on the grounds that Wheeling and Dealing Districts have long since had the materials and their youngsters are certainly no more deserving than Zilch students. Receiving the funds, he takes great pains to assure that each teacher receives all the materials and instruction concerning their contents. All teachers are also encouraged to request assistance at any point.

At the end of a semester, Eager evaluates the materials with respect to accomplishing their objectives and is stunned by the results—students have accomplished no more than with the old nonconcept-oriented materials. At this point, Eager determines that teachers have not been using concept-oriented teaching strategies and, hence, have mitigated the effects of the new materials. He prescribes a massive in-service program to train teachers in concept-oriented teaching strategies, complete with a variety of consultants, microteaching, films, and readings, all preceded by a sensitivity marathon to make the teachers more open to the new approaches.

Evaluation at the end of the second semester also shocks Mr. Eager because it again indicates that not only have students shown little gain in accomplishing objectives, compared with the preceding semester's group, but that the carefully planned in-service program also flopped—only a few first-year teachers used any of the concept-oriented teaching strategies. Eager, in disgust, now diverts his energies from trying to successfully implement the program to preparing reports, speeches, and professional articles to justify Zilch School District's purchase of the materials.

What systematic use of the paradigm might have done for Eager and Zilch School District is to give them a perspective on all the variables within the system that would snuff out reform unless they were controlled. Eager correctly diagnosed that the nonconcept-oriented teaching strategies were counteracting the new materials, but his analysis was too limited and his efforts too disconnected. He failed to note, and hence compensate for, how the other components of the curriculum and their corresponding objectives worked against his reforms. Nor did he take into account, and hence cope with, the noneconomic constraints within the system.

He might have found, for example, that principals had not revised their evaluation formats to accommodate the newer teaching procedures; consequently teachers were chastised whenever they were caught conducting concept-oriented classes. Furthermore, parents, uninformed about the new program, reinforced the principals' behavior by frequent calls, complaining that their youngsters weren't learning any "dates or places."

At the elementary level, Eager might have learned (hopefully, not to his complete surprise!) that the teachers, already knee-deep in time-demanding programs on the "new" math, the "new" science, the "new" reading, plus a few "old" subjects, just didn't have much time left to cope with the demands of the "new" social studies.

In short, the paradigm might have suggested an analytical process, which should have enabled Eager to examine a broader range of interrelated variables than just social-studies curricular materials and to diagnose what other components of the system had to be controlled before he could effect reform in social studies. Furthermore, once Eager had completed his analysis of the system's components, he would have had ready information-bases for generating reforms in other curricular areas.

CONCLUSION

As curriculum shapers increasingly sharpen their focus upon the psychological dimensions of instruction in the social studies, the phenomena of concept learning is likely to take on greater importance. Admittedly, throughout the decade of the sixties, concept learning has not lacked rhetorical emphasis; in fact, considerable evidence suggests that the ever expanding rituals associated with social studies teaching now include professing allegiance to "concept learning." That such a ritual act may be a necessity, Parsons and Shaftel have observed, "is evidenced by the amount of concern which teachers and curriculum workers express over proper statement-making; that the act, once having been made, is discrete and self-satisfying is indicated by its irrelevance to the organization and content of the usual social studies programs."[12] The key issue to be entertained is whether substantial empirical evidence, commensurate with the rhetoric, has been generated to support existing schema for concept learning in social-studies curricula throughout the United States. To this writer, the literature clearly reflects a dearth of experimentally verified conclusions.

It has been said, too, by some social-studies educators, that the decade of the seventies will see our curricular focus shift to affective concerns, since they represent an area "whose time has come." Since concept learning has traditionally been dichotomized as a cognitive process, a further assumption might be that attention will shift from this area and that the important empirical questions will remain unanswered. It may be argued, however, that significant affective variables appear to be attached to the concept-learning process, and precisely those affective social issues that are currently of most concern to our society are intertwined with the ways in which youngsters have learned to categorize objects and events. Stereotyping, for example, may be seen as a special form of concept learning.

[12] Theodore W. Parsons and Fannie R. Shaftel, "Thinking and Inquiry: Some Critical Issues," *Effective Thinking in the Social Studies, 37th Yearbook,* Jean Fair and Fannie R. Shaftel, eds. (Washington, D.C.: National Council for the Social Studies, 1967), p. 124.

A final observation is that the area of social-studies concept learning is likely to be seen increasingly as too important an educational concern to be left to social-studies educators and curriculum specialists. More involvement of psychologists and educational psychologists in research activities appears certain and is highly desirable, because they provide needed expertise for grappling with the empirical issues that remain.

Appendix

Where they are applicable, answers and/or comparative comments are now provided for the exercises in Chapter 8. In addition, a model for evaluating different dimensions of concept learning is suggested.

A CATEGORIZING GAME

List of Social-Science Concepts for Older Students

The following are sample-social science concepts that may be used in playing the game with upper-elementary and secondary students. They are arranged alphabetically.

administration	Congress	election	law
agency	constitution	empire	legislature
aristocracy	continent	enemy	minority
bank	corporation	era	money
barbarian	council	expert	neighborhood
boundary	country	factory	norm
budget	county	family	obligation
business	court	government	obscenity
cabinet	crisis	home	policeman
campaign	culture	humanitarian	region
century	demagogue	individualist	revolution
citizen	democracy	institution	society
colony	depression	isolationist	traitor
committee	economy	jingoist	treaty

List of Social-Science Concepts for Young Children

The following list of items has been used with a variety of classes and has proved to be sufficiently challenging with preschool to early primary groups. Note that the items have been arranged from left to right in order of increasing difficulty; that is, pupils have indicated that terms toward the end of the list are harder to categorize.

banana	dog	window	grandfather
flower	cup	book	policeman
chair	ant	television set	Santa Claus
sock	plant	teeth	principal
hamburger	lump of sugar	ocean	president
rug	refrigerator	light	sky

Transcript of a Game Session

To illustrate how this game may reveal some of the students' problems in categorizing basic concepts, a short section of a classroom transcript is included. Several of the youngsters are unable to classify phenomena that are common to them. In this session the teacher does not know the students' names, and the group is playing the game for the first time. The transcript picks up after the children have been briefed on "taking turns" and are listening, while waiting for their turn. As the dialog begins, the teacher is explaining the rules, after which each of the class, in turn, is given an item for a response.

Teacher Here's how the game goes. It's called "Would you like to be . . . ." and it's a pretend game, where I ask you if you would like to be something, and then you have to tell me, "Yes, I would like to be . . . ." or "No, I would not like to be . . . ." That's easy, isn't it? "Yes, I would like to be . . . ." or "No, I would *not* like to be . . . ." Now there is one other rule, because all games have rules. There are certain things that you can do and certain things that you *can't* do in games. You have to answer with a different word than the one that I give you. Let me give you an example. Let me show you how the game is played. OK? Suppose I said, "Would you like to be a carrot?"

Class (Laughter) I would like to be a carrot.

T OK, then you would answer, "Yes, I would like to be a"—but you can't say the same word, you can't say "carrot." So, you would have to say something like this, "Yes, I would like to be a *vegetable*." I ask you, "Would you like to be a carrot?," and you say, "Yes, I would like to be a"—can't say carrot— "I would like to be a vegetable."

Class (laughter and talking)

T Let me try one more example; let me show you one more, and I'll start to ask each one of you, "Would you like to be . . . ." Everybody is going to get asked. Would you like to be a pencil?

Class Ummm.

T Umm. Yes, and what could you say?

Student Yes, I want to be a . . .

T You can't say "pencil," can you?

S   . . . a piece of paper.

T   Oh, but a pencil isn't a piece of paper, is it? It has to be the *same* thing, only a different word. What would you say?

S   I would like to be a piece of wood.

T   OK, yes, "I would like to be a piece of wood." Well, a pencil is a piece of wood, isn't it—with lead down the middle? Or you could say, "Yes, I would like to be something that you write with." That's right, too, isn't it?

Class   (Nods and verbal agreements)

T   Very good, now you all know how to play the game. That's fine; you are doing very well, because lots of times it's very hard to learn the rules to a game. Let's hurry now and get on with the game. Remember, too, not to tell anyone the answer. Let them try and figure it out themselves. OK, we'll start with the first one. Would you like to be a banana?

S   No, I would not like to be a fruit.

T   Very good. Would you like to be a flower?

S   Uh, uh, no, I would not like to be a plant.

T   Very good. Would you like to be a chair?

S   No, I would not like to be a sitting thing.

T   "No, I would not like to be something that you sit in or a sitting thing." Very good. Would you like to be a sock?

S   No, I would not like to be something that you wear.

T   "Something that you wear." Would you like to be a hamburger?

Class   (Laughter)

S   No, I would not like to be something that you eat.

T   "Something that you eat." Would you like to be a rug?

S   No, I would not.

T   . . . like to be . . .

S   . . . walked on.

T   "Something that you walk on" Very good. Would you like to be a television set?

S   No, I would not like to be a television.

T   Oh, you can't say the same word, remember?

S   Oh, I forgot.

T   No, you would not like to be . . .

S   (No response)

T   Let me ask you the question again, while you are thinking. Would you like to be a television set? That's a hard one.

S   I don't know.

T   OK, how about if we go on to someone else, and then we will come back and ask you another one?

S   OK.

T   Would you like to be a dog?

S   (Long pause)

T   Think it would be fun to be a dog? (pause) What kinds of things are dogs? (pause) What is another name for a dog?

Class   (Students are whispering to one another, and saying aloud, "I know.")

T   Where do you sometimes buy dogs?

S   Store.

T   What kind of store? A special kind of store, isn't it?

S   (Long pause)

T   Well, it could be a *pet* store. So, you might like to be a pet.

S   Yah, I would like to be a pet.

T   That's another name for a dog, isn't it—a pet. OK, let's see if the rest of these boys and girls have been thinking about being a television set. Who shall I ask first? Would you like to be a television set?

S   (No answer)

T   Let's ask somebody else, and then we'll come back and give you another one.

T   Would you like to be a television set?

S   Yes, I would like to be something that you watch.

T   Very good. Let's come back to these two people and give them another turn before we move on. Would you like to be an orange?

S   No, I would not like to be a vegetable.

T   Well, an orange is not a vegetable, it's a fruit. But that's pretty close. Would you like to be a celery stick?

S   I would like to be a flower.

T   But a celery stick is not a flower. It has to be the same thing as celery.

S   (No answer)

T   Let's try another one. Would you like to be a ball?

S   No . . .

T   What is a ball? (pause) What do you do with balls?

S   You play with them.

T   OK, you would not like to be something that you play with. Now we have a new one. This is going to be a hard one. Remember to listen, class, and try to answer to yourself quietly—to yourself. Would *you* like to be a cup?

S   Yes, I would like to be something that you drink out of.

T   You would like to be something that you drink out of. OK. Would you like to be a refrigerator?

S   (No answer)

T   We'll give you another one. Would you like to be a table?

Class   (Laughter)

T   Remember to say, "Yes, I would . . ." or "No, I would not . . . ."

S   (No answer)

T   OK, you think about table, and we will come back and ask you about table again. Would you like to be a refrigerator?

S   No, I would not like to be something that you freeze in.

T She would not like to be something that you freeze in. Very good. Would you like to be a book?

S Yes, I would like to be something that you read.

T Fine. Would you like to be teeth?

S Yes . . .

T Yes, you would like to be . . . . Remember you have to use a different word.

S No . . . (Long pause)

T OK, we will try another one. Would you like to be an apple?

S No, I would not like to be an apple.

T No, you can't say the same word. What do you call apples and bananas?

S (No answer)

T We will come back later then, and give you another turn. Let's ask somebody over here. Would *you* like to be teeth?

S Yes, I would like to be something that's in your mouth.

T That's right, isn't it. Teeth are in your mouth. Would you like to be an ant?

S No, I would not like to be something that bites you.

T Ants do sometimes bite, don't they? Would you like to be a rock?

S No, I would not like to be something that you throw.

T OK, you boys and girls play the game very well. Let's come back to you now. Do you think you have an answer for "table," or do you want to try another one?

S Another one.

T Would you like to be . . . ah, water?

S No, I would not like to be drinked.

T Something that you drink. That's very good. You do drink water. Would you like to be . . . oh, let's see, would you like to be a sweater?

S Yes, I would like to be something that you wear.

T Would you like to be a light?

S No, I would not like to be something that you use to see with.

T Girls, can we have your attention for just a little while longer? Fine. Would you like to be a grandfather?

S No, I would not like to be someone who smokes.

T "Someone who smokes." I'll bet you have a grandfather who smokes. Would you like to be a plant?

S No, I would not like to be something what you grow.

INFERENCE EXERCISE

Country X is, of course, the very real country of Outer Mongolia. Similar profiles may be constructed with the assistance of a basic reference work, such as the *Stateman's Yearbook,* and some supplementary reading. Once Country

X's identity has been verified, it is important to analyze what data in the passage were used to arrive at a solution and *how* the process of verification occurred.

Among the more common strategies used by students to discover the identity of X were (a) look up strange words in the dictionary (country of origin of the item is frequently given), (b) examine a world map, (c) examine an atlas or other reference giving country populations, and, less frequently, (d) list all countries that one can think of and check them systematically in a reference source against the profile of X given.

A LOGIC QUIZ

The validity or invalidity for each of the nine propositions is indicated below.

1. Valid	4. Invalid	7. Valid
2. Invalid	5. Invalid	8. Invalid
3. Valid	6. Valid	9. Valid

Diagrams

1.

Since "Mr. A." *must* be placed in the circle of "winners of acquittal . . .," he *is* one of the "clever lawyers."

2.

Since "this cigarette" may be placed *anywhere* in the circle, "objects on this table," it need *not* follow that it is one of "my cigarettes."

3.

Since "workers" *must* be placed in the circle, "citizens," they *are* "those interested . . . ."

4.

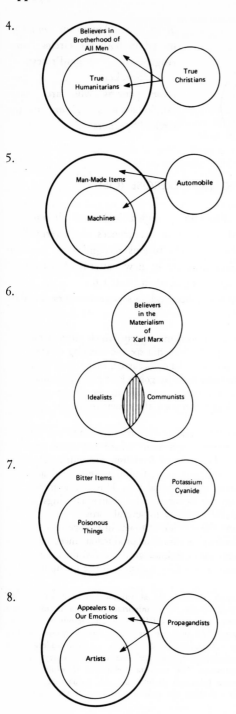

Since "true Christians" may be placed *anywhere* in the circle, "believers . . .," it need *not* follow that they are "true humanitarians."

5.

Since "automobile" may be placed *anywhere* in the circle, "man-made items," it need *not* follow that it is one of the "machines."

6.

Some "communists" *must* be placed in the circle, "idealists," and since *no* "believers . . ." can be placed in the circle, "idealist," *some* "communists" *are* "*non*believers . . . ."

7.

Since "potassium cyanide" *must* be outside the circle of "bitter items," it *is* impossible for it to be one of the "poisonous things."

8.

Since "propagandists" may be placed *anywhere* in the circle, "appealers . . .," it need *not* follow that they are "artists."

Sample Items[5]

1. Given the name of an attribute value, the student can select the example of the attribute value.
2. Given an example of an attribute value, the student can select the name of the attribute value.
3. Given the name of a concept, the student can select the example of the concept.
4. Given the name of a concept, the student can select the nonexample of the concept.
5. Given an example of a concept, the student can select the name of the concept.
6. Given the name of a concept, the student can select the names of the relevant attribute values of the concept.
7. Given the name of a concept, the student can select the names of the irrelevant attributes of the concept.
8. Given the definition of a concept, the student can select the name for the concept.
9. Given the name of a concept, the student can select the correct definition of the concept.
10. Given the name of a concept, the student can select the name of a concept supraordinate to it.
11. Given the name of a concept, the student can select the name of a concept subordinate to it.
12. Given the name of two concepts, the student can select the generalization which relates them.
13. Given a problem, the student can select the correct answer by applying a generalization.

[5] *Ibid.*, pp. 12–21. These items have been taken directly from the report with little or no modification.